Collins

Breeze 2

Semester 2

Collins

Breeze 2

Semester 2

Sonia Duggal
Renu Vishwanath
K.G. Jeyalakshmi
Jyothsna Natraj

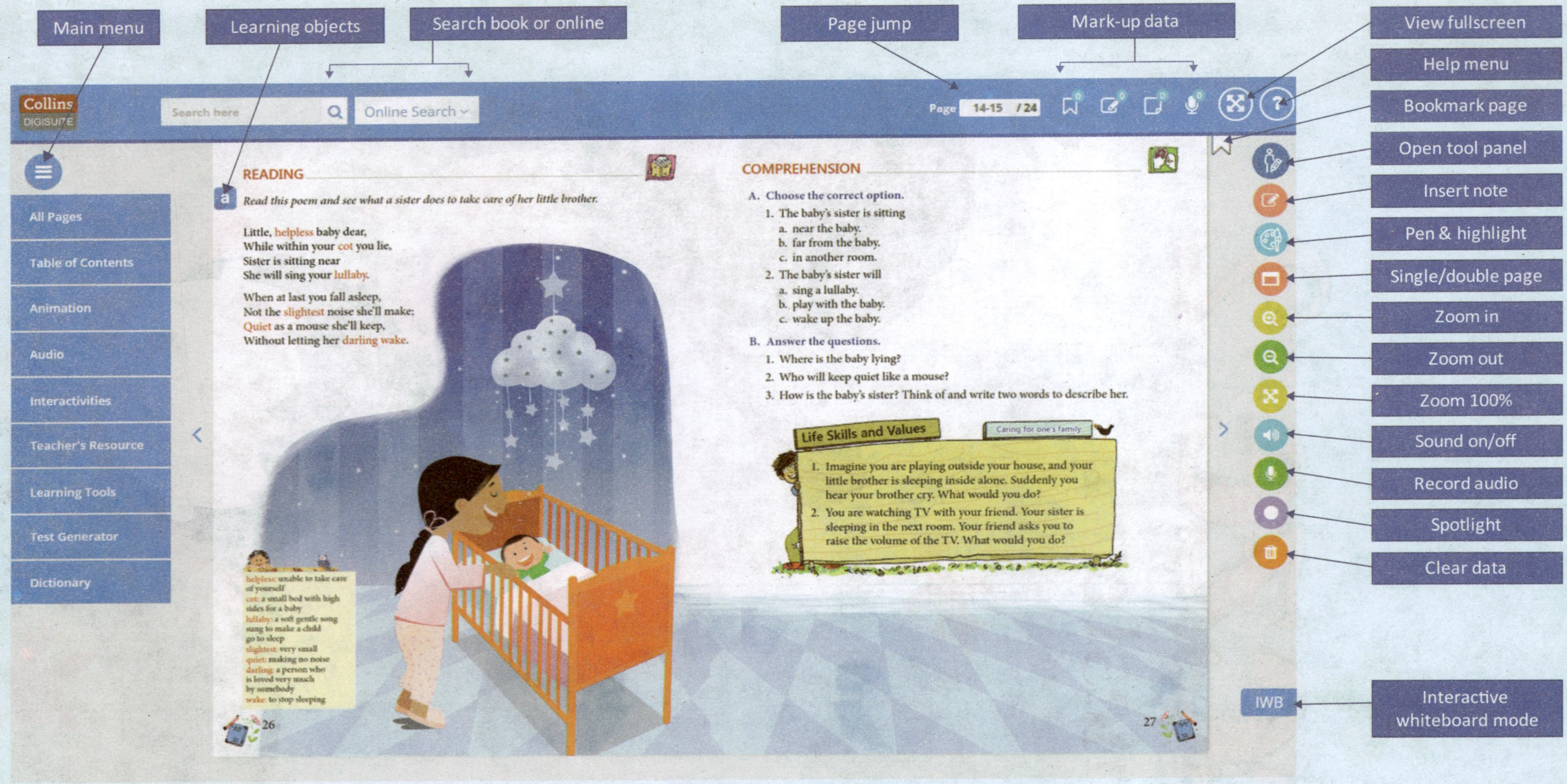

Student + Teacher			Teacher-only	
a animations	**ia** activities	**g** games	**lp** lesson plans	**tn** teacher's notes
ilt instructor-led tutorials	**w** worksheets	**v** videos	**w** worksheets	**ak** answer keys
	audio			

Preface

Breeze—an integrated semester course for classes 1 to 5 provides a comprehensive learning experience. This series of ten semester books teach lessons in an integrated manner, combining all the core subjects—English, Mathematics, Environmental Studies/Science, Social Studies and General Knowledge/Value Education. The lessons facilitate an interactive session in class for the learner's holistic development.

Breeze provides learning experiences with sufficient opportunity for exploration to young minds in their formative stage. The interactive approach of this series integrates multiple intelligences applied in every classroom across all levels.

Cross-curricular links have been created across the areas of learning for experiential and comprehensive development. The enquiry and skill based approach of the books contributes to the trans-disciplinary structure and comprehension. The books maintain a good balance between teacher-led and learner-initiated activities.

Breeze enables learners to understand the interdisciplinary nature of knowledge and apply this approach to problem solving. The well-graded course materials develop a link between natural, cultural and social environment. The course content across the subjects develop basic language skills through analysis, application and appreciation; develop critical and analytical thinking; enhance scientific temperament and create a strong sense of human values.

Some of the pedagogical elements integrated across all subjects include

- Learning Objectives
- Warm up
- New Words
- Do it Yourself
- Think and Answer
- Eco Zone
- Life Skills
- Value Zone
- Activity and Connect for cross-curricular links

Breeze series aims to develop 21st century skills including critical and creative thinking skills, effective communication skills, interpersonal and collaborative skills, and information and media skills in the young learners. This series is supported by comprehensive teacher's resources in the form of an interactive e-book with animations and interactivities, answer keys, lesson plans and a Test Generator for creation of quick test.

We value any feedback on this series. Please e-mail us at schoolmarketing.collins@harpercollins-india.com

Key Features

English

- **Warm-up:** A wide variety of activities at the beginning of chapters to ensure the learners' active engagement in the lesson
- **Reading:** A well-chosen selection of picture stories and comic strips from a wide range of literary genres
- **Comprehension:** Plenty of exercises including factual, inferential and extrapolative questions
- Cross-curricular boxes (*Science Scan, Maths Magic, Earth Speaks, Looking Back, and Fact File*) highlight topics interrelated with other subjects taught in the same grade
- **Glossary:** All new words in the text highlighted and their meanings provided along with a separate glossary for literary devices and literary terms
- **Life Skills and Values:** Separate thematic section on life skills and values
- **Vocabulary:** Boxed explanations of new vocabulary words and topics followed by a variety of exercises
- **Grammar:** Grade-appropriate grammar with detailed explanations and rules in simplelanguage
- **Listening and Speaking:** A wide variety of communicative activities and pronunciation covered in this section
- **Writing:** A well-graded section with a variety of creative-writing exercises including informal and formal letters, diary entries, flow charts, posters, stories, biographies, notices, reports, travelogues, character sketches, book reviews, recipes, acrostic poems, articles, and picture-based compositions
- **Activities:** A fun activity accompanying each poem
- **Projects:** Cross-curricular projects linked to topics taught in the particular grade in other subjects

Mathematics

Concepts explained in simple and easy-to-understand language

- **Exercises and Revision Exercise** within each chapter to recall and revise the concepts learnt
- **Mental Maths** to help practise calculation skills and deductive reasoning
- **Worksheets** to reinforce practice with fun exercises
- **Cross-curricular Links** to integrate knowledge across subjects
- **HOTS (Higher Order Thinking Skills)** and **Challenge** to sharpen the thinking skills beyond textual knowledge
- **Maths Lab Activity** to test skills for investigation, observation and analysis

Environmental Studies

- **Revise and Recall, Think and Answer** test application of the concepts learned.
- **Science in Context** gives interesting extra information on the topic being discussed.
- **Summary** provides snapshot of the chapter content which helps students in quick revision.
- **Cross-curricular learning link** integrates knowledge across subjects.
- **Life Skills** test awareness, empathy and attitude towards self and others.
- Relevant **activities** hone experimental and deduction skills.
- **Project** questions link the concept learned to real-life applications.

Social Studies

- **Observe and Reflect** has pre-reading tasks that allow the learners to infer and relate to the topic.
- **Fact Zone** provides interesting titbits of information and **Find Out** tasks encourage referencing skills.
- **Do It Yourself** contains application-based activities for experiential learning.
- **Eco Zone** sensitizes learners towards conservation of environment.
- **Remember** and **Review Zone** at the end of the units facilitate understanding, recall and reinforcement, and assessment.
- **Think Zone** focuses on Higher Order Thinking Skills.
- **Life Skills Zone** equips learners with the basic skills they need to excel in life and **Value Zone** helps to build the right attitudes and values in learners.
- **Activity Zone** has varied creative tasks.

General Knowledge

- Each task comprises at least two kinds of inputs to help learners arrive at the answers and acquire knowledge at the same time.
- Special themes are an exciting mixed bag of environment education, life skills, values, India, sports, our world, science, language, art, personalities and entertainment to make learners become well-rounded individuals.
- **Activity pages**, aim to hone and cement specific verbal, visual and logical aptitudes through the common lens of general knowledge
- **Life skills**, draws attention to the science behind the safety measures we should take
- **Fact zone**, brings a good dose of fun to learning
- **India-specific content**

Value Education

- **Discuss** are warm up exercises, **Think and Say** are situations to test the application of the value taught and **Read Along** provides a story or poem related to the value being discussed in the chapter
- **Be smart** are exercises based on multiple intelligences
- **Remember** provides brief pointers that the learners can incorporate in their behaviour
- **Figure Out** are questions based on the story or poem taught and **Relate** are real life situations for problem solving
- **Create** provides creative tasks, **Enjoy** suggests media that communicates the value discussed, **Project** provides projects based on the values taught

Acknowledgements

English

The publishers wish to thank and acknowledge the following for granting us permission to use copyright material:

The Water Seed by Munda Writers' Group, translated by Amrit Mishra, illustrated by Ramani Ranjan Sarangi (© Pratham Books, 2014) published by Pratham Books under a CC BY 4.0 license on StoryWeaver.

The publishers have applied for permission for *The Bird of Mind* by Sayan Chaudhuri adapted as *Piklu and the Mynah, Tyltyl's Adventure* by Swapna Dutta.

Every effort has been made to trace copyright holders and to obtain their permission for the use of copyright material. However, in some instances, we have been unable to trace the owners of the copyright pieces published here. The authors and publishers will gladly receive any information enabling them to rectify any error or omission in subsequent editions.

Images and Photographs

Tigatelu, bandian1122; VasjaKoman, TECHDESIGNWORK, Tigatelu; bennyb, kbeis, TECHDESIGNWORK, Lonely__; draco77, Nina_Piankova; lushik, 9comeback, RedlineVector; snapgalleria, rahulpathak, Pazhyna, aqabiz, pinnacleanimates; AlexBrylov, AM29, vishnurajan; vchal, RamonBerk, Claudiad; ksenya_savva; Premiumstock, nicholashan, MarianVejcik; Davidtalukdar, OksanaKiian, bdspn, miroslav_1, jutka5; mlharing, davidevison, Danielrao; P2007.

All other illustrations by Danish Zaidi.

Environmental Studies

All illustrations AptaraCorp Ltd.

Images

saiko3p, Alexandra Lande; Bragin Alexey, vidguten, OlegSam, bogdan ionescu, Siim Sepp, Luciano Mortula; SeDmi, sigur, Tyler Boyes; Imfoto, Boykung; Anita Patterson Peppers.

General Knowledge

All illustrations Henu Studio

Images

pixel107, vm2002, graphic-bee, MarkRyanDesigns, vm2002, subodhsathe, indiaphotos, Vijender Singh-GettyImages/Mail Today The India Today Group; Sushil Kumar-GettyImages/TOSHIFUMI KITAMURA; Saina Nehwal-GettyImages/NOAH SEELAM, Abhinav Bindra-GettyImages/AFP.

Contents

English

Mathematics

Environmental Studies

General Knowledge

VALUE EDUCATION

ENGLISH

1 Tyltyl's Adventure

Courage and Adventure

OBJECTIVES

In this chapter, we will

- *read the story of a sea turtle.*
- *learn to use words with two or more meanings.*
- *learn to use position words or prepositions.*
- *listen to a story and mark sentences as true or false.*
- *play dumb charades and speak about animal movements.*
- *write a story about an animal.*

WARM-UP

Fill in the blanks with the name of the movements for each of the animals.

crawl *fly* *hop* *slither* *swim* *trot*

1. ....

2. ....

3. ....

4. ....

5. ....

6. ....

READING

A mother turtle laid some eggs on the seashore. The eggs hatched and baby turtles crawled out. Among them was Tyltyl, the little baby turtle. He led his brothers and sisters towards the sea. Read on to know what happened to the baby turtles.

Science Scan

- A female sea turtle lays almost 150 eggs every two or three years.
- Sea turtles' eggs look like ping pong balls.
- Sea turtles have excellent eyesight and sense of smell.
- Sea turtles can live up to 80 years.

sunbeams: rays of the sun
heap: an untidy pile
wriggled: moved twisting and turning quickly
restless: (here) the water in the sea is always moving
buried: covered completely in sand
craned: stretched out (the neck)
dizzy: a feeling that everything is turning around and you are going to fall

It was a bright and sunny day. The sunbeams fell on the seashore. They touched the dancing waves. They fell on the fishermen taking out their boats. They fell on the sand heap by the rocks.

The sunbeams made the sand very warm. Suddenly something moved and wriggled under it.

A tiny creature with a soft shell on its back crawled out of the sand. It was Tyltyl, the baby sea-turtle.

Tyltyl was Topsy's baby. Topsy lived in the sea. But the sea is a restless place to live in. So, when it was time for her to lay eggs, she swam back to the shore. She crawled along the sand looking for a quiet place till she found a lovely corner by the rocks.

Topsy laid her eggs, buried them in the sand and swam back to the sea. The sun warmed the sand and kept the eggs warm until it was time for the baby turtles to come out. The eggs cracked and the turtle babies crawled out of the sand.

Tyltyl craned his tiny neck and looked about him. Bright sunlight shone into his eyes making him feel dizzy for a moment. He heard the roar of the sea and the sound of waves breaking over the sand. The sea was calling him!

Five more baby turtles crawled out of the sand. They were his brothers and sisters.

'Hello!' they said looking at Tyltyl.

'Hello!' replied Tyltyl, 'Come, follow me. We don't have much time.'

'Where are we going?' asked one of them.

'To the sea, of course,' said Tyltyl.

Tyltyl led the little group across the sand. A few more turtle babies joined them. Topsy had laid nearly fifty eggs. But some of them did not get enough warmth from the sand. So they were not ready to come out. Some others had been dug up by a naughty boy who took them home.

'Keep by the rocks,' warned Tyltyl. 'Look at those big seabirds flying above. They look very bad! I hope they don't attack us.'

Before Tyltyl could finish speaking, one of the birds swooped down on them. 'Get inside your shells! Quick!' cried Tyltyl. But it was too late. A seagull grabbed one of them and flew away. They felt very sad.

'Just be careful, all of you,' said Tyltyl.

'How far is the sea?' asked one of his brothers.

'I'm hungry and thirsty too,' said another.

'There are some tiny worms here,' said Tyltyl, sniffing inside a sand heap, 'And there's water in that puddle.'

'How far is the sea?' asked a sister of Tyltyl.

'Not too far, I guess,' replied Tytyl.

'I hope there are no more killer birds,' said the youngest of the group.

They crawled along slowly. A group of seagulls tried to get at them once more. But this time they quickly got inside their shells.

swooped: came down suddenly to attack
seagull: a bird with long wings that lives near the sea
sniffing: smelling
puddle: a small amount of water collected at a place
killer: a person or animal that kills

The sound of the sea grew louder. The sand beneath their feet felt wetter.

They were in the water now. But they were not fully safe yet. There came a shoal of big fish looking at them hungrily. 'Hide under those shells! Quick!' cried Tyltyl.

They ducked under a pile of empty shells just in time. Tyltyl looked around anxiously.

'Life seems to be hard,' said one of his brothers. 'It seems to me that we are always hiding from killers of one kind or another!'

'Life is an adventure, silly!' said Tyltyl. 'We'll all get used to it in time. And enjoy it too.'

The big fish were all gone after a while. The water looked blue. It felt as soft as silk. The sound of waves produced music. 'All clear now,' said Tyltyl in a happy voice. 'We have reached home!'

shoal: a group (of fish)
ducked: bent down
anxiously: in a worried manner
adventure: an unusual, exciting and dangerous activity

COMPREHENSION

A. Mark the sentences as true (T) or false (F).

1. Topsy laid her eggs, buried them in the sand and swam back to the sea. ☐
2. Tyltyl had only two brothers and sisters. ☐
3. Tytyl led the other baby sea turtles to the sea. ☐
4. The seagulls picked up two turtles. ☐
5. The sea turtles saved themselves from the seagulls by hiding inside their shells. ☐

B. Answer the questions.

1. How many eggs did Topsy lay?
2. Where did Topsy lay her eggs?
3. What kept the eggs warm?
4. Who was Tyltyl?

5. What did Tyltyl hear when he came out of the egg?
6. When did Tyltyl feel dizzy?
7. Why did Tyltyl tell the sea turtles to keep by the rocks?
8. What was the danger in the sea?

Life Skills and Values

Thoughtfulness and courage

1. Do you think the boy did the right thing by digging up the eggs and taking them home? Why/Why not?
2. If you were a sea turtle and faced similar dangers as Tyltyl, would you see your life as an adventure? Why/Why not?

VOCABULARY

Words with two or more meanings

- Many words in English have two or more meanings. For example:

  Tyltyl craned his tiny neck.

  Cranes usually fly in groups.

  In the first sentence, crane means *to stretch out the neck.*

  In the second sentence, cranes are types of birds.

  A crane is also a tall machine with a long arm used to lift and move very heavy things.

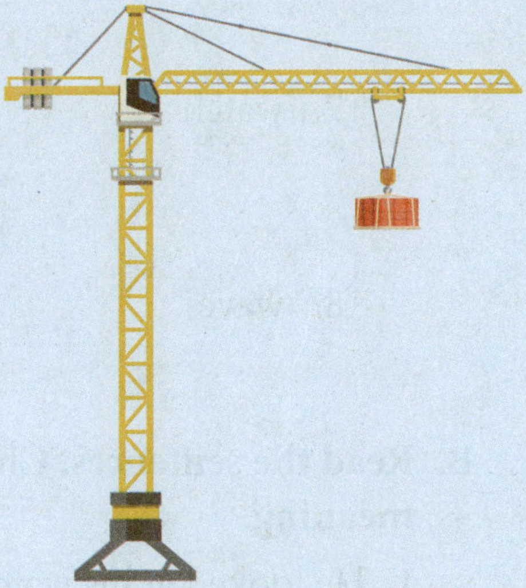

- Here is another example:

  They ducked under a pile of empty shells just in time.

  I saw a duck near the pond.

  In the first sentence, duck means to *bend down.*

  Duck is also the name of a bird.

A. **Read the following words. One meaning of the word is given. Find and match the second meaning.**

Word	Meaning 1	Meaning 2
1. bark	the sound a dog makes	to move one's hand side to side
2. bat	an animal with wings	a circular band
3. can	to be able to	a container
4. light	a lamp	the outer covering of a tree
5. play	to do things for pleasure, as a child	a type of small clock worn on the wrist
6. ring	the sound of a bell	a drama
7. watch	to look carefully	a piece of wood with a handle used to play cricket
8. wave	a raised line of water	easy to lift/not heavy

B. **Read the sentences. Check the meaning in the above table and tick the correct meaning.**

1. He looked at his <u>watch</u> and realised that he was late for school.
   a. Meaning 1 b. Meaning 2
2. When the bell <u>rings</u>, the children run to the playground.
   a. Meaning 1 b. Meaning 2
3. He filled the <u>can</u> with water and took it home.
   a. Meaning 1
   b. Meaning 2

4. He heard the dogs bark all night.
   a. Meaning 1 b. Meaning 2
5. The bat was feeding milk to its baby.
   a. Meaning 1 b. Meaning 2
6. She waved goodbye to her friends.
   a. Meaning 1 b. Meaning 2
7. The bag is very light; I can carry it easily.
   a. Meaning 1 b. Meaning 2
8. The class presented a play on the stage.
   a. Meaning 1 b. Meaning 2

GRAMMAR

Position words or prepositions

- A **preposition** connects a noun or pronoun to other words in a sentence and shows the relationship between them.
- Some prepositions show where something is. For example:

  Topsy lived in the sea.
  Tyltyl led the little group across the sand.

  Where did Topsy live? *In* the sea.
  Where did Tytyl lead the little group? *Across* the sand.
- *In* shows a relation between the sea and Topsy. Topsy lives inside the sea.
- *Across* show a relation between sand and Tytyl.
- Here are some more examples:

  The book is on the table.
  The clothes are in the cupboard.
  The garden is behind the house.
- Some more prepositions are:

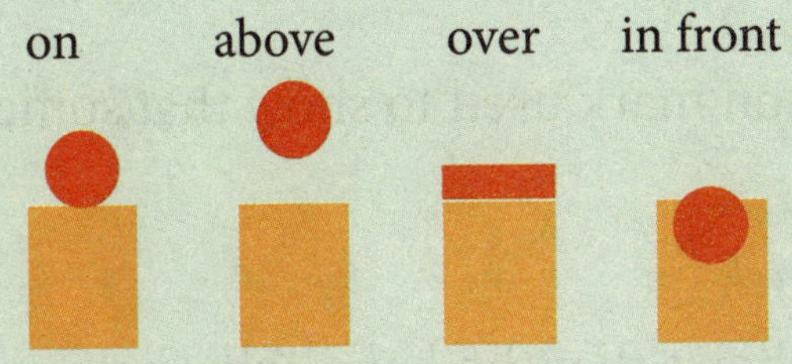

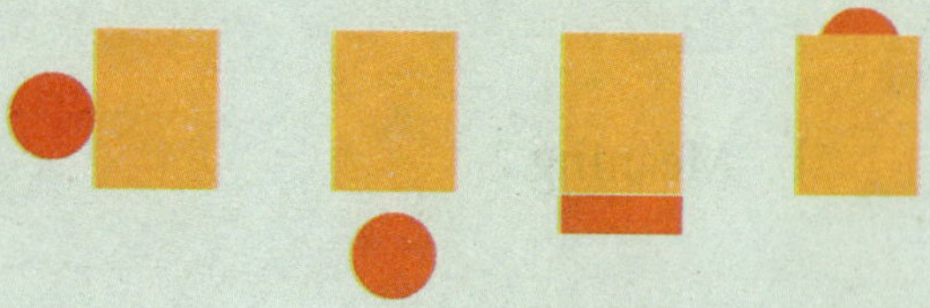

beside below under behind

A. Look at the picture carefully and fill in the correct prepositions.

1. The cat is .... (*in*/*on*) the roof.
2. The girl is .... (*in*/*on*) the house.
3. The car is .... (*behind*/*beside*) the house.
4. The dog is .... (*in front of*/*under*) the house.
5. The cow is standing .... (*behind*/*inside*) the house.
6. The cat is standing .... (*beside*/*under*) the chimney.

Apostrophe (')

- The **apostrophe** (') is a small punctuation mark used to show that something belongs to somebody. For example:

  Tyltyl was Topsy's baby.

  In the above sentence, the apostrophe shows that the *baby Tyltyl* belongs to *Topsy*.

- Here are some more examples:

  Tina's school bag is beautiful. (The school bag belongs to Tina.)

  Raj's bat is heavy. (The bat belongs to Raj.)

  My grandmother's house is very big. (The house belongs to my grandmother.)

B. Put the missing apostrophe in each sentence.

1. Your cats tail is short.
2. Ratnas son is in school.
3. Zoyas brother is very kind.
4. Bobbys rabbit eats carrots.
5. My sisters shoes are white.
6. The elephants trunk is long.
7. Mitas bicycle is under the tree.
8. Aryas lunch box was lost yesterday.

LISTENING AND SPEAKING

Listening

A. Listen to the passage carefully. Then mark the sentences as true (T) or false (F).

1. Meera went to the beach in the morning. ☐
2. She found some empty shells lying on the sand. ☐
3. She did not pick up any shells. ☐
4. Some seagulls flew over Meera's head. ☐
5. The seagulls did not harm Meera. ☐

Speaking

B. Work in groups of 10. Write the words below on separate pieces of paper. One student in the group picks up a slip and acts out the movement. The others guess the name of the animal and the word for the movement. Then say a sentence using the word.

crawl	*flutter*	*fly*	*gallop*	*hop*	*jump*
prowl	*slither*	*trot*	*waddle*		

WRITING

Think of any animal. Then complete these sentences to write a story about it.

One day I went to the garden. I saw .... (name of your animal) *It was* .... (describe the animal) *At first I was very scared but* ....(name of the animal) *was very kind. I took it home. I gave it* ....
.... (name of foods) *to eat and* .... *to drink.*
I named it .... (name given to the animal).
We became friends.

• 2 How Many Seconds in a Minute?

Time

OBJECTIVES

In this chapter, we will:
- *read and enjoy a poem.*
- *learn about action words and use them in sentences.*
- *learn to make a toy clock.*

WARM-UP

Look at the time and draw hands on the clocks.

READING

Read the poem by Christina Georgina Rossetti and see whether you know the answers to questions on time.

Fact File

- Have you ever wondered why the moon has different sizes on different nights?
- The moon goes round the Earth. It takes the moon four weeks or one month to complete one round.

How many seconds in a minute?
Sixty, and no more in it.

How many minutes in an hour?
Sixty for sun and shower.

How many hours in a day?
Twenty-four for work and play.

How many days in a week?
Seven, both to hear and speak.

How many weeks in a month?
Four, as the swift moon runneth.

How many months in a year?
Twelve, the almanack makes clear.

How many years in an age?
One hundred says the sage.

How many ages in time?
No one knows the rhyme.

shower: rain
swift: moving very quickly
runneth: old English spelling for runs
almanack: (also spelled *almanac*) an annual calendar containing important dates and information about important activities, etc.
sage: a very wise person

COMPREHENSION

A. Read the poem again and fill in the blanks.

1. There are .... seconds in a minute.
2. There are .... minutes in an hour.
3. There are .... hours in a day.
4. There are .... weeks in a month.
5. Nobody knows how many .... there are in time.

B. Answer the questions.

1. What does the movement of the moon determine?
2. What makes it clear that a year has twelve months?
3. Who says one age has hundred years?

Life Skills and Values

Punctuality and routine

1. *Being punctual* means *being on time*. Do you think it is important to be punctual? Why/Why not?
2. Do you think we should always follow a fixed routine? Why/Why not?

VOCABULARY

Action words

- *Work*, *play*, *hear*, and *speak* are all **action words** that are used in the poem. The words that define actions are called **action words**.
- Here are some more examples.
  laugh *play* *run* *paint* *sing*

A. Choose the action word in each set and circle it.

1. beautiful	rose	smell
2. boys	cry	flowers
3. cook	grandma	stove
4. dance	men	people
5. dog	kitten	bark
6. paint	picture	words
7. poem	poet	read
8. girls	shout	voice

B. Describe your day and fill the time in the clock. You can use the action words given in the box.

eat	*go*	*leave*	*play*	*read*	*sleep*	*wake up*	*watch*

1. I .... at 

2. I .... to school at 

3. I .... at 

4. I .... school at 

5. I .... at 

6. I .... at 

7. I .... at 

8. I ....at 

ACTIVITY

Make a clock using a paper plate.

Directions:

Colour the hands of the clock as per the colour key. Cut out the hands and clock face. Use a paper fastener to attach the hands to the face. Make sure the hands turn freely. Then glue the clock face onto a paper plate.

Make Your Own Clock

Minute Hand
Colour Red

Hour Hand
Colour Blue

3 Piklu and the Mynah

Empathy for Animals

OBJECTIVES

In this chapter, we will:

- *read a story of a boy who loves birds.*
- *learn about synonyms, and giving feelings to non-human things.*
- *learn to understand and use simple present and present continuous tenses.*
- *listen to a description and identify animals.*
- *express our thoughts through pictures and words.*
- *write our daily routine using the simple present form of the given action words.*

WARM-UP

Look at the two sets of pictures carefully. Which set do you like better? Why? Share your thoughts by completing the sentence given below.

Picture Set A

Picture Set B

I like the picture set .... because ....

....

....

READING

Piklu is always restless to meet the birds in the garden. He loves nature and birds. But one day he sees a bird in a cage. Read this translation of a Bengali story by Bimalendra Chakraborty to find out what Piklu does.

Summer holidays are here! Piklu doesn't have to go to school. Still he wakes up early in the morning.

Rubbing his eyes he comes out in the garden. He is restless to hear the chirping of birds and to see them. His eyes begin to search the garden for them. At a careful glance he is able to spot a magpie, a sparrow, a bulbul, a parrot and many other birds.

One by one they greet him. Piklu begins to count them, 'One… two… three…' He moves further. Suddenly two yellow-beaked mynahs fly over his head.

Piklu becomes happy. He claps his hands with joy. The flowers swing their heads as if nodding in happiness. He can hear the bees humming cheerfully. Piklu plays with the birds all day long. He bathes them and feeds them too.

Next morning, Piklu sees a small mynah fluttering in a bird cage hanging from a tree. Its legs are tied to a chain. He is

restless: unable to relax
chirping: (of a bird) making short and sharp sounds
glance: look
spot: find
magpie: a long-tailed crow
bulbul: a songbird with a melodious voice
mynahs: small birds with a loud call
fluttering: (of a bird) flapping the wings quickly

shocked to see this. Piklu runs to his mother and asks, 'Who has caged the poor mynah, Ma?' He learns that his elder brother Toton caught it in the nearby forest.

Fact File

- The mynah's calls include chirps, clicks, croaks, and whistles.
- Mynahs are often caged because they can be trained to speak and even sing.

Piklu notices that the bird is sad and does not eat anything. Once in a while it gives out a sad cry. Piklu too feels sad for the bird. Hearing the mynah cry, no other bird comes to the garden. He wonders what to do. Then an idea **strikes** his mind! He brings a chair, climbs on it to reach the cage and **unlocks** it.

Piklu opens the chain tied to its leg and **caresses** the bird softly. Then he calls his mother who comes with an ointment. Mother **applies** some ointment to the bird's wounded leg.

Mynah feels better and chirps at Piklu. He lovingly **teases** Mynah and teaches her to say his name. Soon Myhnah learns to say, 'Pik-lu... Pik-lu'. Next, Mynah climbs up to a tree, and jumps from one branch to another. Finally she flies higher and higher into the **vast expanse** of the blue sky.

The red sun shines on the eastern sky. The flowers of the garden are blessed with the morning light. **Dragonflies** dance around. Bees and butterflies flutter over the colourful flowers. All of them are very happy.

But Piklu is worried. Will the Mynah find her mother? Does she know the way to her home?

strikes: (here) a thought that comes to mind suddenly
unlocks: opens
caresses: touches gently
applies: puts
teases: (here) touches playfully
vast expanse: something that is spread out
dragonflies: fast-flying insects with two pairs of large transparent wings

Next morning, Piklu hears someone calling him by his name. He rushes out. Mynah is sitting with its mother on the branch of a *tagar* tree.

Piklu shouts with joy! Toton also comes out hearing his voice. He looks at the happy mynah. He feels sorry for putting it in a cage. He promises never to cage a bird in future.

Fact File

- *Tagar* is a flowering shrub found commonly throughout Southeast Asia.
- It is called the pinwheel flower in English because of its pinwheeled-shaped petals.
- It is known as *Chandni* in Hindi and *Nandiar Vattai* in Tamil.
- Parts of the plant are used to make medicines.

COMPREHENSION

A. Choose the correct option.

1. Every morning Piklu wakes up and searches for .... in the garden.
   a. birds
   b. animals
   c. friends
2. .... fly over Piklu's heads.
   a. Mynahs
   b. Two yellow beaked Shaliks
   c. Sparrows
3. When Piklu sees the bird in the cage,
   a. he is sad.
   b. he is shocked.
   c. he gives it water.
4. Hearing the Mynah cry,
   a. all birds gather around the crying bird.
   b. its mother comes to meet her baby.
   c. no other birds come to the garden.

5. Piklu shouts with joy because
    a. his mother gets an ointment.
    b. the mynah comes to meet him.
    c. Toton promises never to cage a bird in future.

B. Answer the questions.

1. What does Piklu search for every morning?
2. Name three birds that Piklu finds in the garden.
3. Who puts the bird in the cage?
4. Where did the person get the bird from?
5. How did the bird show its unhappiness?
6. How did Piklu help the bird?
7. Who came back the next day? What was Piklu's reaction?
8. How does Toton feel when he looks at the happy mynah?

Life Skills and Values

Empathy for animals

1. Do you think it is right to cage animals and birds? Why/Why not?
2. Do you think all animals and birds have a language of their own which they use to talk with each other? Would you like to learn it? Why/Why not?

VOCABULARY

Synonyms

- Read these word pairs.

    simple – easy   *big – large*

- Two words in each word pair mean the same. Such words are called **synonyms**.

A. Read the following words. Two of the words mean the same in each row. Circle them.

1. afraid bold scared timid
2. cat gift present skirt
3. clean dirty fresh tidy
4. easy hard rich simple
5. fast quick slow stroll
6. murmur shout speak whisper

Giving feelings to non-human things

- Sometimes we give feelings to things, plants and animals.
- It is also sometimes an extension of how we feel. For example:

  The wind howled loudly.

B. Read the following sentences. Underline the non-human thing and the action it does.

1. The alarm clock shouted at me.
2. Rita heard the cake calling her.
3. A house is a friend that protects me.
4. The moon played hide-and-seek with the clouds.

GRAMMAR

Simple Present Tense

- The **simple present tense** is used to state facts. For example:

  He *wakes* up early in the morning.

  Piklu *claps* his hands with joy.

  Mynah *moves* to the garden to climb up to a tree.

  The words *wakes*, *claps*, and *moves* are action words.

  They tell us about an action which happens regularly.

  The words are said to be in the simple present tense.
- The following chart describes how to use the simple present tense.
  - Add *-s* to most verbs

- Add *-es* to verbs that end in *-ch*, *-o*, *-s*, *-sh*, *-x*, and *-z*. For example: *watches, does, kisses, washes, fixes, buzzes*

Positive sentence	
I	*go* (verb)
You	
They	
We	
He	*goes* (verb + *es*)
She	
It	

Negative sentence		
I	*do not* ('do' verb + not)	*go* (verb)
You		
They		
We		
He	*does not* (do + es + not)	*go* (verb)
She		
It		

For example:

Piklu wakes up early. He goes to the garden.

His mother reads the newspaper. She goes to the office.

I/ They/ You go to school every day.

A. Read the following sentences. Fill in the blanks with the correct form of the action words given in the brackets.

1. We .... (*eat*) dinner together.
2. Mr Mann .... (*fly*) an aeroplane.
3. They .... (*play*) tennis every day.
4. The sun .... (*rise*) in the east.
5. Tina .... (*write*) with her left hand.

Present continuous tense

- We use the **present continuous** to refer to actions or events that are happening at the moment of speaking. For example:

  You *are reading* the textbook.

  The teacher *is speaking.*

  Everyone *is studying.*

- The present continuous is formed by adding *am/is/are* and *-ing* to action words.

- The following chart describes how to use the present continuous tense.

Positive sentence		
I	*am*	*playing (verb+ing)*
You	*are*	
He/She	*is*	
It	*is*	
They	*are*	
We	*are*	

Negative sentence			
I	*am*	*not*	*playing (verb+ing)*
You	*are*		
He/She	*is*		
It	*is*		
They	*are*		
We	*are*		

B. Read the following sentences. Fill in the blanks with the correct option.

1. Sona .... a storybook.
   a. am reading
   b. are reading
   c. is reading
2. Tara and Shreya .... for a holiday.
   a. am going
   b. are going
   c. is going
3. I .... with my toys.
   a. am playing
   b. are playing
   c. is playing
4. They .... dinner together.
   a. am cooking
   b. are cooking
   c. is cooking
5. We .... a movie.
   a. am watching
   b. are watching
   c. is watching

LISTENING AND SPEAKING

Listening

A. Listen to the description. Guess the name of the animal/ bird/insect and circle it.

1. butterfly
2. duck
3. frog
4. mouse
5. spider
6. dog

Speaking

B. Show and Tell

What kind of a world do you want to live in? Draw pictures and share your thoughts.

WRITING

Write your daily routine using the simple present form of action words given in the box.

brush	*eat*	*go*	*play*	*read*	*study*	*take*	*wake*	*watch*

I wake *up at 7 o'clock.*

Then I ....

After that I ....

....

When I come back from school, I ....

....

In the evening, ...

....

At night, I ....

....

Finally, ...

....

....

4 The Water Seed

Courage and Adventure

OBJECTIVES

In this chapter, we will:

- *read a story of a young man who helps his village find water.*
- *learn to make and use compound words in a sentence.*
- *learn the past simple and the past continuous tenses.*
- *listen and fill in the blanks.*
- *do picture-reading and narrate a story using past tense.*
- *learn to write an acrostic poem.*

WARM-UP

Have you ever wondered where water comes from? Look at the pictures given below. Unscramble the words to discover the sources of water.

1. VRIRE ....

2. NSWO ....

3. EAKL ....

4. NIAR ....

READING

When the rains do not come in the village, the young men go in search of water. One of them comes back with a water seed! Read on and find out what happens next.

Long ago, in a village it did not rain for three years.

The earth was parched and all the plants dried up. The dry dust blew into people's eyes. They were very worried. They knew they could not live without water.

The village chief called for a meeting. Old and young, everybody came.

The chief asked four young men to come up.

He said, 'I want the four of you to go in four different directions to find water.'

parched: very dry due to hot weather and no rains
worried: unhappy or troubled about problems that might happen in the future

Three of them returned after some days, as they could not walk any further. The fourth one, who had gone north, reached a white mountain.

As he climbed up the slippery slope, he saw a cave. There was an old lady in the cave. 'Where can I find water?' the man asked her.

The old lady said, 'Go higher up on the mountain.'

The man climbed right to the top. He broke off a piece from the white mountain. He wrapped it carefully in a sack.

Earth Speaks

- We can find water under the ground.
- This water comes mostly from rain, melted snow, and other water that seep through soil, sand, or the cracks in the ground.
- Due to gravity, the water just keeps moving downward, underneath the Earth's surface, until it can't go any farther.
- Sometimes, groundwater can seep back up to the surface in the form of springs and wetlands.

He ran back to the village as fast as he could.

When he got there, everyone ran to him to see what he got. He was very tired but happy. He said, 'I've brought back the water seed.'

When he opened his sack, the ice had melted into water! It dripped on to the ground and was absorbed by the soil.

With a cry, the villagers started digging to get back the water seed. They dug and they dug deeper. At last, they struck water!

slippery: something smooth, wet or oily and is therefore difficult to walk on or to hold
wrapped: covered in paper or soft material
dripped: water fell in small drops
absorbed: took in or soaked up (here, the soil took in the water)
struck: (here) found

Everyone shouted with joy, 'The water seed has given us water! The water seed has given us water!' And now the village had water.

They looked after it well. Now the village has water even if it does not rain.

COMPREHENSION

A. Choose the correct option.

1. It did not rain for
   a. one year.
   b. two years.
   c. three years.
2. .... came for the meeting called by the village chief.
   a. Everybody
   b. Only old people
   c. Only young people
3. The young man met .... in the cave.
   a. bear
   b. snow
   c. an old lady
4. The young man brought back .... from the mountains.
   a. a plant seed
   b. the old lady
   c. a water seed
5. When the villagers dug the ground, they found
   a. water.
   b. snow.
   c. a water seed.

B. Answer the questions.

1. What had happened to the earth and plants in the village?
2. Why were the people worried?
3. What did the village chief ask the four men to do?
4. Where did the fourth man go?
5. What did the old lady tell him?

6. What did the man get from the mountain?
7. What happened when the man opened the sack?
8. Why did the villagers shout with joy?

Life Skills and Values

Courage and community

1. Imagine there is a flood in a neighbouring town, and people are stuck in their homes without water or food. What would you do to help these people?
2. Would you want to become a commando or a soldier, where you might need to jump from flying helicopters, dive into deep oceans, or climb high mountains to protect the country? Give reasons for your answer.

VOCABULARY

Compound words

- **Compound words** are single words that are formed by joining two different words. For example:

black + board → blackboard *pea + nut → peanut*

A. Use words from the word box to make compound words. The pictures will help you.

bow *brush* *bug* *fish* *man*

1. jelly + ... → ....

2. lady + ... → ....

3. rain + ... → ....

4. snow + ... → ....

5. tooth + ... → ....

B. Fill in the blanks with the compound words that you have made.

1. I use my .... to clean my teeth.
2. A bright red .... sat on the leaf.
3. It is fun to make a .... on a snowy day.
4. You can't have a .... without a little rain.
5. .... live in the sea and are found in all oceans.

GRAMMAR

Simple Past Tense

- We use the **simple past tense** to talk about things or actions which happened sometime in the past.
- The past could mean *an hour ago, yesterday, last night, two months ago, three years ago*, etc.
- In many cases, the simple past is formed by adding *–ed* to the verb. For example:

  clean — cleaned *play — played* *walk — walked*

  I cleaned my room last Sunday.

  I walked to the park and played with my friends.

- But some verbs do not follow the *–ed* rule. For example:

verb	*past tense*
bring	*brought*
buy	*bought*
catch	*caught*
come	*came*
do	*did*
give	*gave*
go	*went*
have	*had*

verb	*past tense*
is	*was*
meet	*met*
see	*saw*
sell	*sold*
sit	*sat*
teach	*taught*
win	*won*
write	*wrote*

- Some verbs remain the same in their simple past form. For example:

verb	*past tense*
cost	*cost*
cut	*cut*
hit	*hit*
hurt	*hurt*

verb	*past tense*
put	*put*
read	*read*
shut	*shut*
spread	*spread*

A. Read the following sentences from the story. Underline the verbs in the simple past tense.

1. All the plants dried up.
2. The village chief called for a meeting.
3. The man climbed right to the top.
4. He broke off a piece from the white mountain.
5. He wrapped it carefully in a sack.
6. He was very tired but happy.
7. It dripped on to the ground and was absorbed by the soil.
8. Everyone shouted with joy.

B. Fill in the blanks with the simple past form of the verbs in brackets.

1. It .... (*rain*) yesterday.
2. My mother .... (*lock*) the door.
3. Soha .... (*clean*) the blackboard.
4. I .... (*play*) with my friends this morning.
5. Ram .... (*give*) him a ball for his birthday.
6. She .... (*go*) to her uncle's house in holidays.
7. Everybody .... (*sit*) quietly to watch the play.
8. My friends.......................... (*come*) to my house last Saturday.

Past Continuous Tense

- We use the **past continuous** tense to talk about an action that was happening continually in the past.
- The past continuous is formed with *was* or *were* and the *–ing* form of the verb. For example:

  I was sleeping when it started to rain.

  Last night at 8 o'clock we were watching a movie.

C. Fill in the blanks with the past continuous form of the verbs in brackets.

1. She .... *(run)* to school.
2. It .... *(rain)* all morning.
3. They .... *(sit)* under a tree.
4. We .... *(stand)* in the snow.
5. Anna .... *(watch)* television.
6. Radha .... *(talk)* on the phone.
7. He .... *(write)* a letter to his father.
8. The birds .... *(fly)* around the garden.

LISTENING AND SPEAKING

Listening

A. Listen to a short paragraph on the importance of water. Then fill in the blanks.

1. We need water for .... and ....
   (*Mention any two things.*)
2. .... per cent of the earth is covered by water.
3. Only .... per cent water is fresh and usable. The rest of the water is .... or is in the form of ....
4. We .... (*should/should not*) save water.

Speaking

B. Divide your class into seven groups. Each group gets a picture postcard and discusses the picture amongst themselves. Then each group briefly describes their picture to the class. Make sure the group presentation is in the same order as the pictures appear here.

1.

3.

2.

4.

5. 

6. 

WRITING

Acrostic poem

- Poems are of different kinds.
- In an acrostic poem, the lines are formed by the first letters of the chosen word. For example:

Water on the rug,
Around the house and above!
Till the roof and in my cup,
Everywhere on the earth!
Run! Run! Run! It's a flood! It's a flood!

Write an acrostic poem with any one of the following words.

- TREE
- ANIMALS
- EARTH

....

....

....

....

....

....

....

5 Ismat's Eid

Compassion and Humour

OBJECTIVES

In this chapter, we will:

- *read the story of a man who cares for his family very much.*
- *learn to use opposite words.*
- *learn about homophones and use them in sentences.*
- *learn to use the joining words and and but.*
- *listen and extract information.*
- *play roles and enact the play.*
- *learn to write a thank-you note.*

WARM-UP

Festivals are a time to celebrate, connect and bond with others. Guess the names of the following festivals and fill in the crossword.

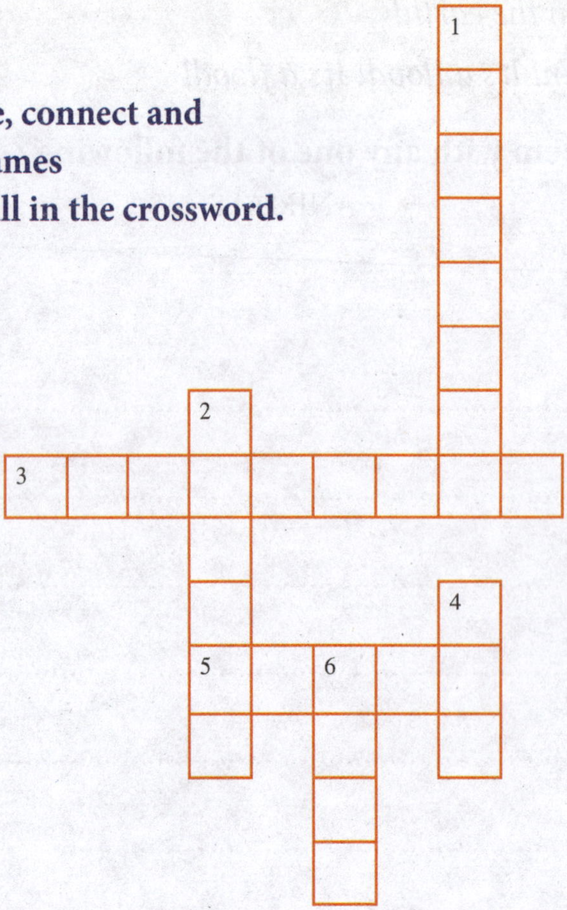

Across:

3. 

5. 

Down:

1. 

2. 

4. 

6. 

READING

Ismat, a cobbler, is a kind man. He decides to buy special gifts for his family for Eid. The shopkeeper insists that he buys something for himself too. But the trousers the shopkeeper shows are too long for Ismat. But they can be shortened, can't they? Read on to see what happens.

Narrator: Ismat, the cobbler, was very busy. It was Eid next day. People were trying out new shoes. They were all sold out.

Ismat: Ah! At last I can go and buy some gifts for my family.

Narrator: Ismat went to the shop of Hamza.

Hamza: Salam! How can I help you?

Ismat: Salam! I want to buy my wife a new *burqa* for Eid!

Hamza: Okay, give me a minute, please.

Ismat: Also show me a *dupatta* for my *ammi* and bangles for my daughter.

Hamza: How about this bright blue *dupatta* with beads? And look at these red and green bangles.

Ismat: Wonderful! My family will be very happy.

Hamza: What about you? Your trousers have patches. Why don't you buy yourself a new pair?

Ismat: Ah! Perhaps I will.

Hamza: Look at this one. Only one is left.

Ismat: But it's four fingers too long. Could you shorten them for me, Hamza?

Fact File

- Eid is also known as Eid al-Fitr.
- It is celebrated at the end of Ramadan, the month of fasting when people eat only one meal a day.
- On Eid, people wear new clothes, visit and exchange gifts with their friends and family, and eat special sweet foods.
- People go to a mosque and offer prayers. It is also a time for sharing joy with family and friends and caring for the poor.

cobbler: a person who makes shoes and other footwear as a profession
Eid: a Muslim festival
salam: an Urdu greeting
burqa: a long, loose garment covering the whole body from head to feet, worn by Muslim women
dupatta: a long piece of cloth worn around the head and neck by women
beads: small pieces of glass, wood, etc. that are sewn on to fabric or threaded to make jewellery
patches: pieces of cloth sewn on to clothes to cover holes in them

Hamza: I'm sorry. I have to get ready for Eid.
Why don't you ask your wife?

Ismat: Good idea!

Narrator: Ismat goes back home with all the gifts.

Yasmeen: This is beautiful. I love the *burqa*.
Did you get anything for yourself?

Ismat: Yes, a pair of trousers but they are four fingers too long. Could you shorten them for me, please?

Yasmeen: Sorry, I don't have time. I have to make *biryani*.
Why don't you ask your mother?

Narrator: Ismat goes to his mother.

Ismat: *Ammi*, I have bought you this lovely *dupatta* for Eid. Do you like it?

Habiba: Wow, this is so beautiful! I love the colour.
Did you get anything for yourself?

Ismat: Yes, a pair of trousers but they are four fingers too long. Could you shorten them for me?

Habiba: I have no time. I have to make *sheer korma*.
Why don't you ask Mahjabeen?

Narrator: Ismat goes to his daughter.

Ismat: Mahjabeen, I have brought you a gift.

Mahjabeen: These bangles are so *lovely*, *Abba*.
Did you get anything for yourself?

Ismat: Yes, look at these.

Narrator: Mahjabeen looks at the trousers.

Mahjabeen: *Abbu*, they look a little too long.

Ismat: Could you shorten them for me?

Mahjabeen: I'm sorry, *Abbu*. Not today.
I have to make *samosas* and take care of the baby.

biryani: a dish made from rice with meat, fish or vegetables
sheer korma: pudding made with vermicelli, dates and milk
lovely: beautiful; attractive

Ismat (to himself): Okay. I will do it myself.

Narrator: Ismat took a pair of scissors and cut a few inches from the bottom of the trousers and hemmed up the edges. He put the trousers on a table and went out to visit the poor and the sick and give them money for Eid.

Habiba (as she stirred the *sheer korma*): Ismat is such a good son. I must shorten his trousers.

Narrator: Habiba cuts off four inches from the trouser bottoms and hems them. She folds the trousers and puts them back on the table.

Yasmeen: Ismat is such a good husband. I must shorten his trousers.

Narrator: Yasmeen cuts off four inches from the trouser bottoms, hems them, folds them and keeps them back on the table.

hemmed: folded the edges and sewed them
stirred: moved it using a spoon, etc.

Mahjabeen (as she was frying the samosas): *Abbu* is such a kind father! I must shorten his trousers.

Narrator: Mahjabeen cuts off four inches from the trouser bottoms, hems them, folds them and keeps them back on the table.

Narrator: Next day it is Eid. Suddenly, a loud noise comes from the bedroom and all the three women go running.

Ismat: Ohhhhhh! Aaaah! Ya Allah!

Yasmeen, Habiba and Mahjabeen (worried): What happened? Is everything okay?

Narrator: Ismat steps out of his room. His new trousers hung up to his knees!

Yasmeen: I shortened them by four fingers only.

Habiba: I, too, shortened them by four fingers.

Mahjabeen: I also shortened them by four fingers.

Narrator: And everybody burst out laughing.

Yasmeen, Habiba and Mahjabeen (together): Let's all sew the pieces back.

Narrator: One by one, they sewed the pieces back. Finally, everybody was dressed in their new Eid clothes and off they went to the mosque.

COMPREHENSION

A. Answer the questions.

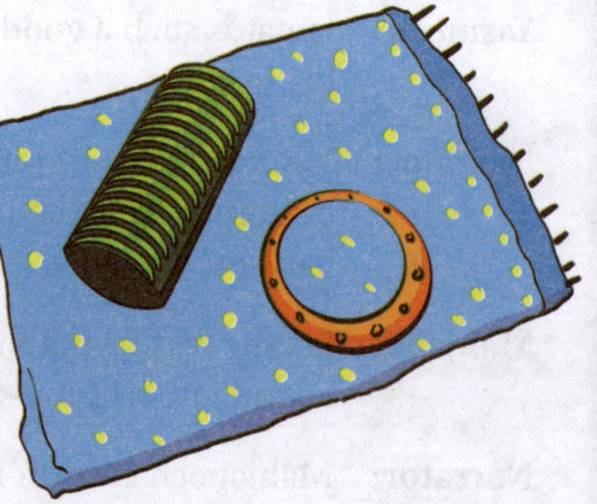

1. Why did Ismat buy gifts for his family?
2. What did Ismat buy for his wife?
3. What did Ismat buy for his mother?
4. What did Ismat ask his wife?
5. What was his wife making?
6. What did Ismat decide to do with his trousers?
7. Why did Ismat go to the poor and the sick?
8. What happened to Ismat's trousers?

B. Read the lines from the play and answer the questions.

1. *Your trousers have patches.*
   Why don't you buy yourself a new pair?
   a. Who is speaking?
   b. Whose trousers have patches?
2. *This is beautiful. I love the burqa.*
   a. Who is speaking?
   b. What is beautiful?
3. *What happened? Is everything okay?*
   a. Who are the speakers?
   b. Who are they talking to?

Life Skills and Values

Caring and sharing

1. Why is it important to care for one's family?
2. What would you gift your parents on a festival even if you did not have any money to buy anything?

VOCABULARY

Opposites

- **Opposites** are words that mean things as different from each other as possible. For example, *bad* is the opposite of *good*.

more – less	*buy – sell*	*cry – laugh*
happy – sad	*small – big*	*win – lose*

A. Choose the opposites of the underlined words from the box and fill in the blanks.

cheap	*noisy*	*old*	*opens*	*out*	*soft*

1. The rock is hard but the feather is ....
2. The woman was .... but the man was young.
3. Every time I close the door, the dog .... it with his paw.
4. Everybody was very quiet in the house but it was very .... outside.
5. We got in through the front door and came .... from the back door.
6. She thought that the dress was expensive but it was actually ....

Homophones

- **Homophones** are words that have the same sound but different spellings. For example:

  I want to buy my wife a burqa for Eid.

I shortened them by four fingers.

In the above sentence, *buy* means to purchase something, while *by* is a preposition that shows the length there.

- Here are some more examples:

  I have only one pencil.

  I won the match easily.

In the above sentence, *one* is a number, while *won* refers to winning in the past.

B. Circle the correct homophone and complete the sentence.

1. He .... (*ate/eight*) an apple.
2. The sky is clear and .... (*blew/blue*).
3. The whale lives in the .... (*sea/see*).
4. The .... (*son/sun*) is shining brightly.
5. There was a .... (*be/bee*) sitting on the flower.
6. There are .... (*too/two*) umbrellas in the cupboard.
7. We spent the .... (*hole/whole*) day cleaning the garden.
8. I am going to my grandparents' place for a .... (*weak/week*).

GRAMMAR

Joining words: *and* and *but*

- **Joining words** are words that join two words or sentences together.
- We use *and* to join two words or sentences. For example:

  Ismat bought a dupatta for his ammi.

  Ismat bought bangles for his daughter.

  To join the sentences together, we can say:

  Ismat bought a dupatta for his ammi and bangles for his daughter.
- *And* is a joining word.
- We use *but* to join two words or sentences that express opposite ideas. For example:

  The box is big.

  The box is not heavy.

To join the two sentences together, we can say:

The box is big but not heavy.

- *But* is also a joining word.

A. Use the joining word *and* to combine the sentences in each pair. Some other changes may be needed too.

1. Alice fell down. Alice hurt her feet.

   ....

2. Dina wakes up early. Dina goes for walk.

   ....

3. My father baked a cake. My father baked some cookies.

   ....

4. Arya will eat pasta for lunch. Arya will eat bread for lunch.

   ....

5. Ram helped Shona with homework. Ram helped Vidhi with homework.

   ....

B. Use the joining word *but* to combine the sentences in each pair. Some other changes may be needed too.

1. Meenu is short. Rahul is tall.

   ....

2. The TV is on. No one is watching it.

   ....

3. Tina likes to sing. She cannot dance.

   ....

4. Radha fell down. She did not get hurt.

....

5. I went to Rahul's house. He was not at home.

....

Punctuation

- We use special marks while writing. These special marks are called **punctuation marks**.
- When we speak, we pause after a complete **sentence**.
- Similarly, when we write we put a **full stop** (.) at the end of a sentence. For example:

  I have an English class today.

Question mark

- When we want to ask for information, we change the way we speak.
- This helps the listener to understand that we are asking a **question**.
- Similarly, when we write a question, we put a **question mark** (?) at the end of a sentence. For example:

  Can I sit here?

  Do we have a holiday tomorrow?

Exclamation mark

- When we express surprise or strong emotion or warning, we change the way we speak.
- Similarly, when we express surprise in writing, we put an **exclamation mark** (!) at the end of a sentence. For example:

  Watch out! There is a car coming.

  Hurray! Our team won the inter-school championship trophy!

C. Read the following sentences. Use a full stop (.) or a question mark (?) or an exclamation mark (!) at the end of each sentence.

1. Is it sunny outside
2. Where is my apple
3. What a beautiful day

4. Who lives in that house
5. Look I have a new dress
6. Can you ride the red bike
7. A bee makes sweet honey
8. I am working on my science project

LISTENING AND SPEAKING

Listening

A. Listen to the descriptions of some festivals carefully and fill in the blanks.

1. Christmas is celebrated by Christians on .... December to honour of the birth of Jesus Christ.
2. Diwali is celebrated by Hindus in the honour of Lord Rama. He came back to Ayodhya on this .... after 14 years of exile.
3. Eid is a Muslim festival on which people exchange .... and pray to God in the mosque.
4. The .... anniversary of Guru Nanak is celebrated as Gurupurab by Sikhs.

Speaking

B. Work in groups of six. Play the roles of the narrator, Hamza, Ismat, Yasmeen, Mahjabeen and Habiba. Read out the play with proper expressions and gestures.

Some points to remember:

- You don't have to memorise the play; you can read out the dialogues.
- Be loud enough and clear.
- Use proper expressions and gestures to make your dialogues more interesting and easier to understand.
- Practise before you read out the play.

WRITING

Complete this thank-you note for any two people you love.

Dear ....,

Thank you for ....

....

I wanted to tell you that ....

....

I think you are ....

because ....

.... *(your name)*

6 The Kite

Travel

OBJECTIVES

In this chapter, we will:
- *read and enjoy a poem.*
- *learn about words related to wind.*
- *spot differences between the two pictures.*

WARM-UP

A. Have you ever wondered how the world looks from top? Unscramble the words and identify the pictures.

1. OMUTANISN .... 2. REIVR .... 3. ICYT ....

B. Did you ever have a chance to look at such places from the top? If so, what did you see and from where? Discuss it in the class.

READING

In this poem, the poet – Frank Dempster Sherman – wishes to become a kite and travel to many places. Let's read and find out where all he wishes to travel.

I often sit and wish that I,
Could be a kite up in the sky.
And ride upon the breeze and go,
Whatever way I chanced to blow.
Then I could look beyond the town,
And see the river winding down.
And follow all the ships that sail,
Like me, before the merry gale.
Until at last with them I came,
To some place with a foreign name.

breeze: a gentle wind
chanced: happened without planning
merry: happy
gale: a very strong wind
foreign: unfamiliar, strange

COMPREHENSION

A. Mark the sentences as true (T) or false (F).

1. The poet wants to ride upon the breeze. ☐
2. The poet wants to look beyond the sailing ships. ☐
3. The poet is afraid to travel to unknown places. ☐
4. In the end, the poet wants to get back home. ☐

B. Answer the questions.

1. What does the poet wish to be?
2. Name three things that the poet would see from the top.
3. Do you think the poet is bored of living in the same place? Why/Why not?

Life Skills and Values

Imagination and travel

1. If you could fly, where would you like to go and why?
2. Do you like visiting new places and meeting new people? Why/Why not?

VOCABULARY

Words related to wind

- Winds are of different kinds.
- The poet in the poem uses words such as *breeze* and *gale* to describe the movement of wind.
- While breeze is *gentle*, gale is *strong*.

A. Match the names of winds with their pictures.

1. Breeze

2. Tornado

3. Storm

B. **Can you find the words from the previous exercise in the word grid given below?**

T	O	R	N	A	D	O
S	T	O	R	M	W	C
H	N	P	U	F	F	Y
I	L	B	L	E	R	G
B	R	E	E	Z	E	A
W	E	R	T	Y	O	L
C	E	C	L	V	G	E

ACTIVITY

Spot eight differences in the two pictures.

7 Travelling to Assam

Travel

OBJECTIVES

In this chapter, we will:

- *read a travelogue on a journey to Assam.*
- *learn to use travel-related words in sentences.*
- *learn the alphabetical order of words starting with the same letter.*
- *learn to use the verbs am, is, are in sentences.*
- *learn to use wh- words to form questions.*
- *listen to a dialogue and extract information.*
- *learn to ask for and give directions.*
- *learn to write in a postcard.*

WARM-UP

What does the word *travel* remind you of? Think about it, discuss and write down the travel-related words in the boxes.

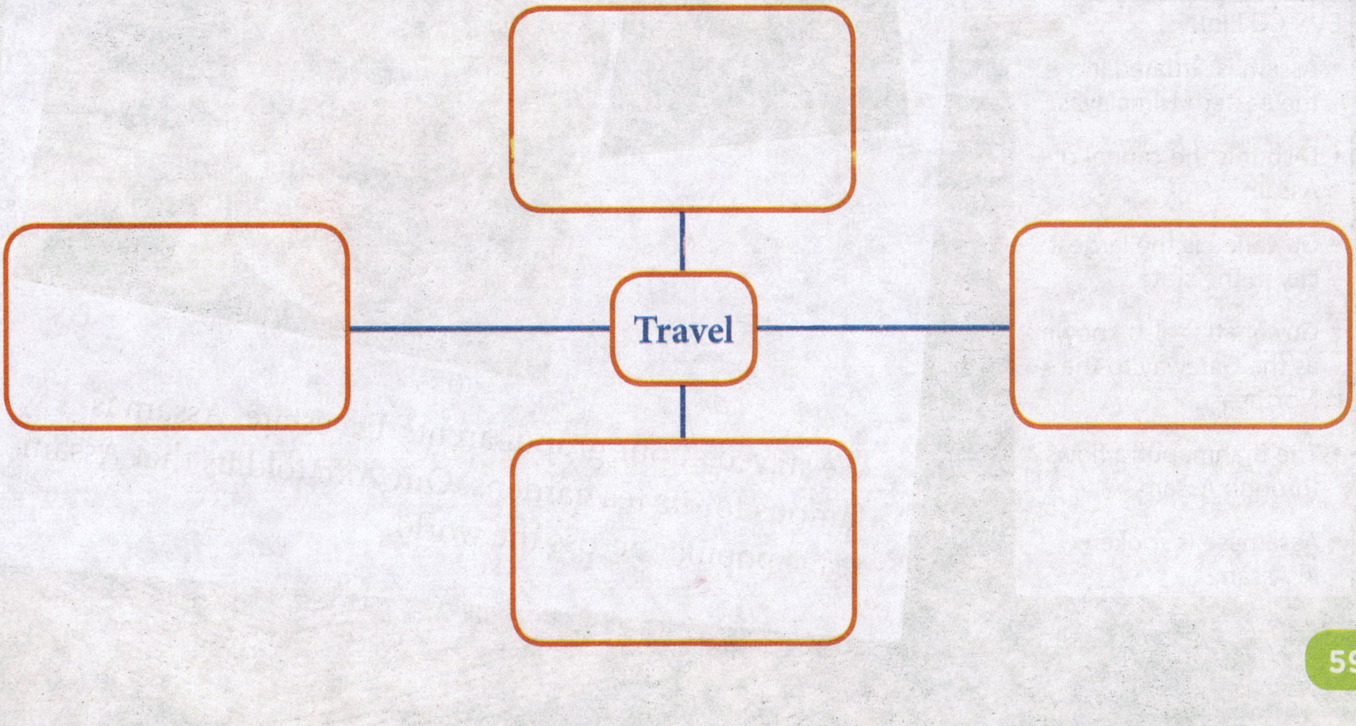

READING

Jahnobi and her brother, Niyor visited their Koka (grandfather) and Aita (grandmother) in the beautiful northeastern state of Assam. Let's look at the scrapbook they created after their trip.

EVS CC Link

- Assam is situated in the eastern Himalayas.
- Dispur is the capital of Assam.
- Guwahati is the largest city in the state.
- Guwahati is also known as the Gateway to the Northeast.
- The Brahmaputra flows through Assam.
- Assamese is spoken in Assam.

We stayed at our grandparents' tea estate. Assam is famous for its tea gardens. Our *Aita* told us that Assam tea is popular across the world.

This is a picture of the *Bohag Bihu* festival we celebrated with our family. It is the main festival of Assam. It is celebrated in the month of April. It marks the Assamese New Year. We sing *Bihu geets* or songs to the beats of the *dhol*. We dance with a *Jappi*, the traditional conical bamboo hat.

We dressed in traditional clothes gifted to us by our grandparents. I wore a *mekhela-chador*. A *mekhela* is a skirt and a *chador* is a long piece of cloth pleated and tucked into the *mekhela*. Niyor wore a *dhoti* and a *gamusa* or a traditional towel.

Our Favourite Assamese Food:
Healthy and tasty!

Masor tenga is fish curry cooked in a broth made with tomato, *outenga* (elephant apple) and lemon. It is eaten with rice.

Aloo pitika is a simple dish eaten with rice and *dal*. It is made of mashed or crushed potatoes mixed with mustard oil, onion, coriander and salt.

Pitha is a snack made of rice. It can be cooked in different ways–sweet or salty, steamed or fried. It is usually eaten during breakfast or evening tea.

Postcards from Assam...

Our day trip to Kaziranga National Park

We rode an elephant and saw a lot of wild animals like the great Indian one-horned rhinoceroses, royal Bengal tigers, and golden langurs.

Weekend trip to Sivasagar

One weekend, we travelled to the town of Sivasagar to see the Rang Ghar. It has Asia's first amphitheatre. In the past, it served as the royal sports building where kings and nobles watched buffalo fights and other sports.

A visit to Guwahati

We also went to Guwahati to pray at the Kamakhya Temple. It was built around 1100 to 1200 years ago!

We also bought beautiful silks, bamboo, and cane products as gifts for our friends back home.

COMPREHENSION

A. Mark the sentences as true (T) or false (F).

1. Assam is situated in South India. ☐
2. Assam is famous for coffee plantations. ☐
3. *Bohag Bihu* celebrates the Assamese New Year. ☐
4. *Aloo Pitika* is eaten with rice and *dal*. ☐

B. Answer the questions.

1. What do women and men wear in Assam?
2. Which river flows through Assam?
3. Where is Rang Ghar located?
4. Name any two dishes of Assam.
5. What do you think makes Assamese food healthy?

Life Skills and Values

Travel

1. Imagine you are going on a holiday and must pack your bag. Make a list of the things you will need, if you were going to each of these places:

   a. beach b. desert c. mountains

VOCABULARY

A. Read the sentences and choose the correct words from the box.

camera	*hotel*	*restaurant*	*suitcase*	*tent*	*train*

1. We pack our things in it. ....
2. While camping, we stay in this. ....
3. While travelling, we usually eat at this place. ....

4. When we go on a holiday, we often stay there. ....
5. We capture memories by clicking pictures with this. ....
6. We sometimes use this means of transport for travelling. ....

B. Use the words in the above exercise to fill in the blanks.

Last summer, we went for a holiday to Shimla by .... We stayed in a .... there. There was a very good .... where we had some Himachali food. We decided to go camping and we packed our clothes in a .... We spent the night in a .... on the foothills of the Himalayas. It was a very nice experience. In the morning, we took a lot of pictures with our .... It was a great holiday.

Alphabetical order of words starting with the same letter

- Read these words:

  train, ticket, tent, torch
- They all begin with *t*.
- To arrange these words in alphabetical order:
  - look at the second letter of each word
  - arrange the words according to the order of the second letter
  - So, the alphabetical order of these words is:

  tent, ticket, torch, train

C. Arrange the words in alphabetical order.

1. land leg lost light

   ....

2. boy bell baby bread

   ....

3. ant apple alligator aeroplane

   ....

4. cot cat crow clip

   ....

5. pit pup plum parrot

....

6. egg eel enemy elephant

....

GRAMMAR

Using *am, is, are*

- We use *am* with the pronoun *I*. For example:

  I am a girl. ***I am*** a boy.

- We use *is* with *he*, *she*, *it* or a naming word that is only one in number. For example:

  *She **is** naughty.* *It **is** my pencil.*

  *My mother **is** a doctor.* *The peacock **is** a beautiful bird.*

- We use *are* with *we*, *you*, or *they* and with naming words which mean more than one in number. For example:

  *We **are** students.* *You **are** smart.*

  *They **are** in the room.* *The children **are** singing.*

A. Fill in the blanks with *am*, *is* or *are*.

1. I .... seven years old.
2. We .... happy today.
3. It .... made of wood.
4. Rita .... my best friend.
5. She .... a Hindi teacher.
6. They .... making a noise.
7. These beds .... comfortable.
8. My grandfather .... a farmer.

Questions with *wh-* words

- We use the ***wh***-words *what*, *where*, *when*, *who*, and *why* to ask questions.
- ***What*** is used to ask about a thing or an action. For example:

  What is on the table? *What are you doing?*

- ***Where*** is used to ask about a place or position. For example:

  Where is the table? *Where are you going?*

- ***When*** is used to ask about the time, day, month, year, etc. For example:

  When do you go to your grandparents' place?

  When do we celebrate Diwali?

- ***Who*** is used to ask about people. For example:

  Who is in the room? *Who is shouting there?*

- ***Why*** is used to ask about the reason for something. For example:

  Why are you sad? *Why is the shop closed today?*

B. Fill in the blanks with the correct question word.

1. .... is in the box?
2. .... are you crying?
3. .... is your father going?
4. .... is your brother's name?
5. .... will make breakfast today?
6. .... are you going for a holiday?
7. .... do you have winter vacation?
8. .... will help you with homework?

C. Fill in the blanks with the most suitable question word and *am, is, are*.

1. Question: .... Mumbai?

   Answer: It's in India.

2. Question: .... on the table?

   Answer: That is my storybook.

3. Question: .... Mr R.N. Kovind?

   Answer: He is the 14th president of India.

4. Question: .... your birthday?

   Answer: It's tomorrow.

5. Question: .... you running?

   Answer: I am late for school.

LISTENING AND SPEAKING

Listening

A. Listen to the conversation and mark the sentences as true (T) or false (F).

1. Mona is going to Nainital during the summer vacation. ☐
2. She is going there with her grandparents. ☐
3. Mona and her family will travel by train. ☐
4. They will live in a small cottage there. ☐
5. They plan to go boating there. ☐

Speaking

B. Work in pairs. Taking turns, ask for and give directions to reach the school library from your classroom.
You can use these clues.

Asking for directions	Giving directions
• *Can you tell me the way to .... from here?* • *Do you know the way to ....?*	• *Go straight.* • *Turn right/ turn left.* • *On the right, you will find .... /on the left you will find ....*

WRITING

Postcard writing

- Postcards are cards with a picture on one side.
- Always think of the person you are writing the postcard to, and choose a picture postcard he/ she would love.
- The back of the postcard is usually split in two. The address and the message are written at the back. We do not write anything in the front.
- Write the receiver's full address on the right side of the postcard, and your message on the left.
- Place the stamp on the top right of the postcard.
- Write the date on the top left side of the postcard.
- Your message needs to fit within the left side of the postcard, and hence must be short and sweet. You may use colourful pens to write a message.
- Sign your name on the bottom left of the postcard. You may also add the name of the place you're writing from.
- Postcards are sent without an envelope.
- Many stationery and gift shops sell postcards. They are also sold everywhere in popular tourist areas.

Write a postcard to your friend who lives in a faraway city. Your message could be about anything. Study the sample below, and recreate a similar postcard in your notebooks.

22 December 2017

Dear Ted,

Today I saw the white desert under the moonlight, and I wish you were here to see how breathtaking it looked! I'll be visiting you this New Year's Eve. See you soon!

Give my love to uncle and aunty!

Love,
Jenny
Rann of Kutch, Gujarat

34, Himkunj Lands
Mazatec Towers, Sector 54
Delhi 112233

PROJECT 2

My Last Holiday

Write a travel journal entry. Write about your last holiday.

The weather was...

I ate...

Five things I did on my holiday...

MATHEMATICS

1 Division

Learning Objectives

- To understand the concept of equal sharing in division
- To understand the relation between multiplication and division

Let's Get Started

Read the following statements.

Mother **shared** the biscuits ***equally*** among her three children.

Teacher **shared** the fruits ***equally*** among the children in the classroom.

In a village, paddy was ***shared equally*** among the people of that village.

EQUAL SHARING

₹6 has to be shared among Sunil, Anil and Lena. First, they take 1 rupee each.

In all these statements, things are shared equally among people. The concept of sharing equally is known as **division**.

Now, they are left with ₹3. Again they take one rupee each.

₹6 is shared equally among 3 people and each one gets ₹2.

6 divided by 3 gives 2.

We write this as 6 ÷ 3 = 2.

Symbol for division ÷

Example 1: Share 12 ice creams equally among 4 students.

Give one ice cream to each student. Then, take the remaining **8** ice creams and again give one to each. Now, you are left with **4** ice creams. Again, give one each. Now, all the **12** ice creams are shared equally among the **4** students, that is, each one gets **3** ice creams.

Student 1 Student 2 Student 3 Student 4

12 divided by 4 gives 3. It can be written as 12 ÷ 4 = 3.

Example 2: Share 10 balloons equally among 2 students.

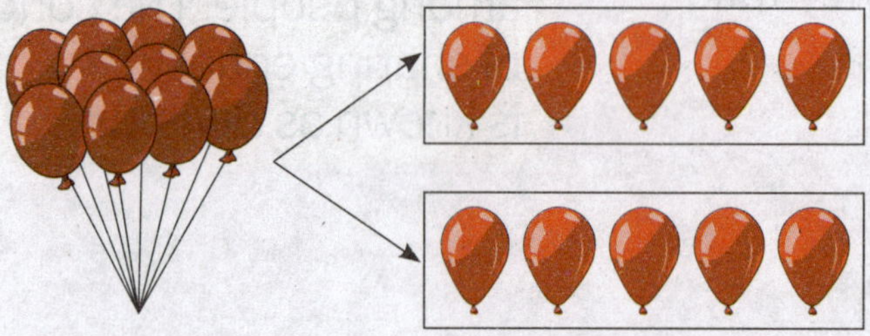

Division fact: 10 ÷ 2 = 5

Exercise 1.1

1 Share the following equally among the given number of people. Also, write the division fact for each.

(a) 12 pencils among 6 people

Division Fact: ______________

(b) 15 rupees among 5 people

Division Fact: ______________

(c) 24 beads among 6 people

Division Fact: ______________

(d) 35 oranges among 7 people

Division Fact: ______________

(e) 21 mangoes among 3 people

Division Fact: __________

(f) 25 ice creams among 5 people

Division Fact: __________

EQUAL GROUPING

Example 1: A shopkeeper has 12 eggs. 2 eggs can be packed in a tray. How many egg trays will he need to pack all 12 eggs?

Take 2 eggs and place them in a tray.

Now, take 2 more eggs and place them in another tray.

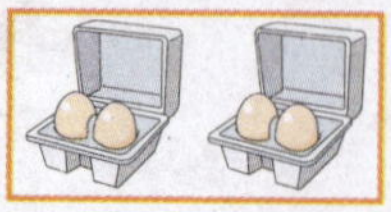

Similarly place all the remaining eggs in the trays.

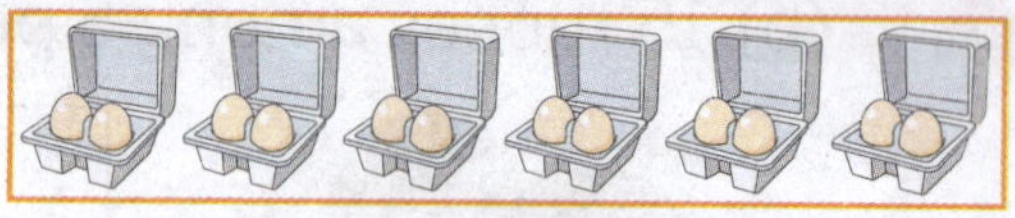

There are no eggs left. Therefore, the shopkeeper will need 6 trays to keep all the 12 eggs. Here, we have divided the number 12 into 6 equal groups of 2 each.

12 divided by 2 is 6.

That is, $12 \div 2 = 6$.

$12 \div 2 = 6$

12 → Total number; 2 → Number in each group; 6 → Number of groups

Example 2: There are 25 apples. A basket can hold 5 apples. How many baskets are required for 25 apples?

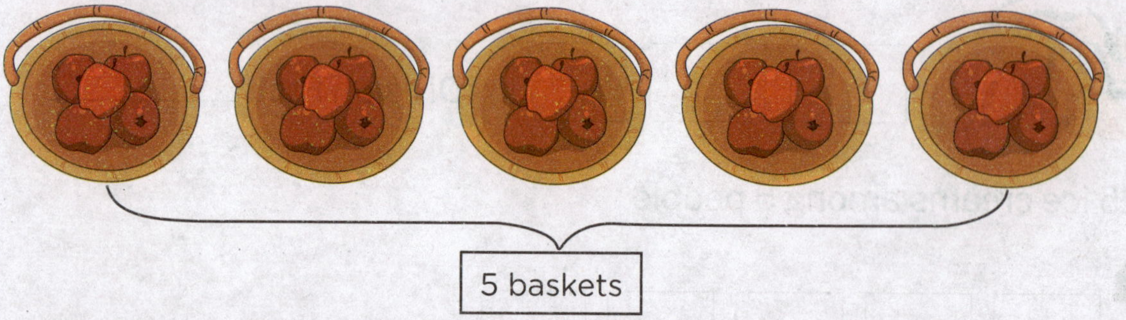

Therefore, a total of 5 baskets will be required to keep all the apples.

That is, $25 \div 5 = 5$.

Exercise 1.2

1 **Find out how many boxes are needed to pack the coffee mugs. Also, write the division fact.**

(a) 10 mugs with 5 mugs in each box Division Fact: ________

Number of boxes needed = ______

(b) 8 mugs with 2 mugs in each box Division Fact: ____________

Number of boxes needed = ______

(c) 15 mugs with 3 mugs in each box Division Fact: ____________

Number of boxes needed = ______

(d) 24 mugs with 3 mugs in each box Division Fact: ________

Number of boxes needed = ______

(e) 40 mugs with 10 mugs in each box Division Fact: __________

Number of boxes needed = ______

(f) 36 mugs with 9 mugs in each box Division Fact: __________

Number of boxes needed = ______

(g) 16 mugs with 8 mugs in each box Division Fact: __________

Number of boxes needed = ______

DIVISION AS REPEATED SUBTRACTION

Division of two numbers can even be done using the method of repeated subtraction. To divide using repeated subtraction, subtract equal groups from the total until you reach 0 and count the number of times you have subtracted.

Example 1: 12 ÷ 2

Here, you need to find how many times 2 can be subtracted to reach 0.

$$\begin{array}{r} 12 \\ -\ 2 \\ \hline 10 \\ -\ 2 \\ \hline 8 \\ -\ 2 \\ \hline 6 \\ -\ 2 \\ \hline 4 \\ -\ 2 \\ \hline 2 \\ -\ 2 \\ \hline 0 \end{array}$$

After subtracting 2 from 12 six times, you reached 0. This means that there are six 2s in 12. Therefore, the division fact is 12 ÷ 2 = 6.

Example 2: 15 ÷ 5

You need to subtract 5 from 15 each time until you get 0.

$$\begin{array}{r} 15 \\ -\ 5 \\ \hline 10 \\ -\ 5 \\ \hline 5 \\ -\ 5 \\ \hline 0 \end{array}$$

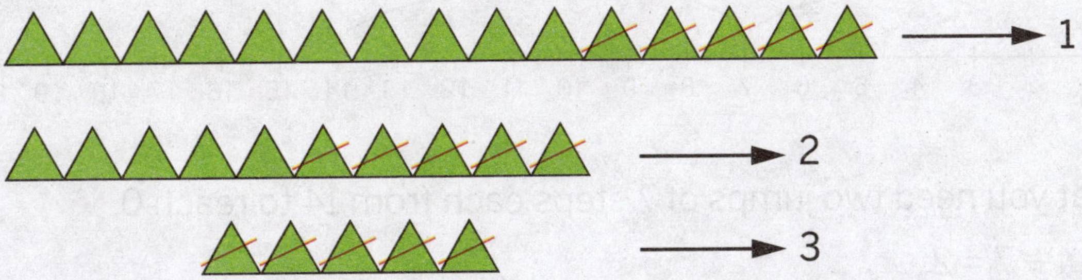

We have subtracted 5 three times. Therefore, the division fact is 15 ÷ 5 = 3.

DIVISION USING NUMBER LINE

Number line can be used to carry out the division of two numbers.

Example 1: 12 ÷ 4

On the number line, make a jump of 4 steps backward from 12. You reach 8.

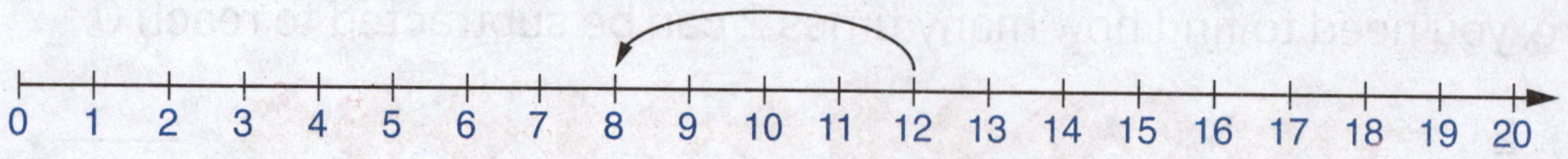

Again make another jump of 4 steps and you reach 4.

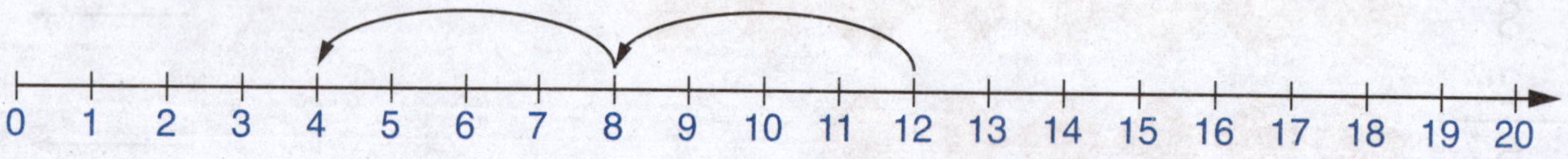

From 4, make a jump of 4 steps to reach 0.

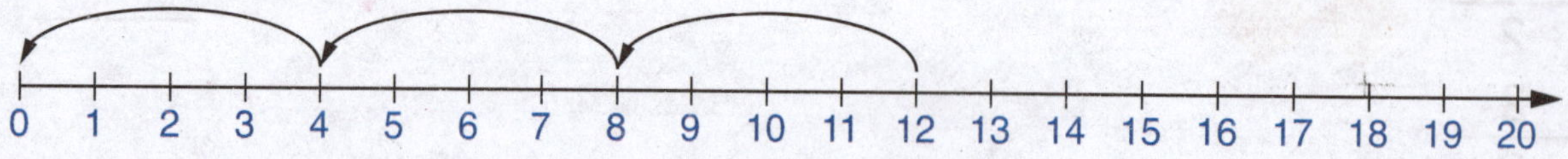

So, you take 3 jumps of 4 steps each to reach 0 from 12. Therefore, 12 ÷ 4 = 3.

Example 2: 14 ÷ 7

Find how many jumps of 7 steps each are required to reach 0.

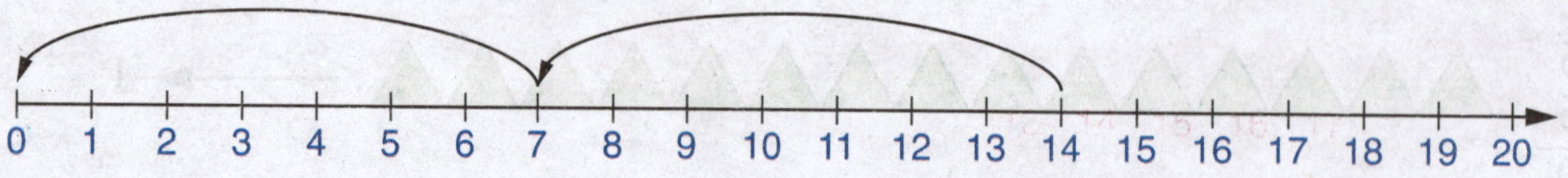

Note that you need two jumps of 7 steps each from 14 to reach 0.

Hence, 14 ÷ 7 = 2.

Exercise 1.3

1 **Solve the division problems using repeated subtraction method and write the division facts.**

(a) 45 ÷ 9 = ______

(b) 28 ÷ 4 = ______

2 **Solve the following division problems using number line.**

(a) 15 ÷ 5 = ______

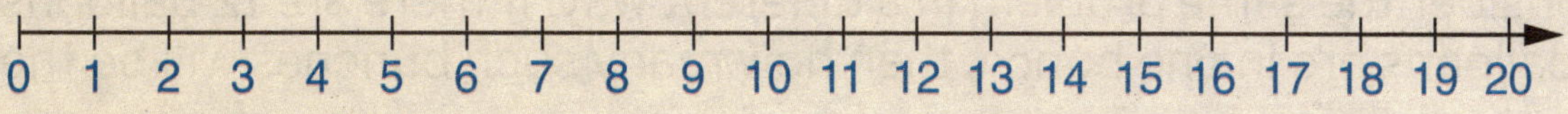

(b) 12 ÷ 6 = ______

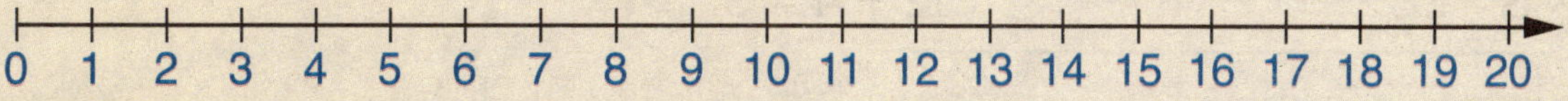

3 **Write the division fact for each number line representation.**

(a)

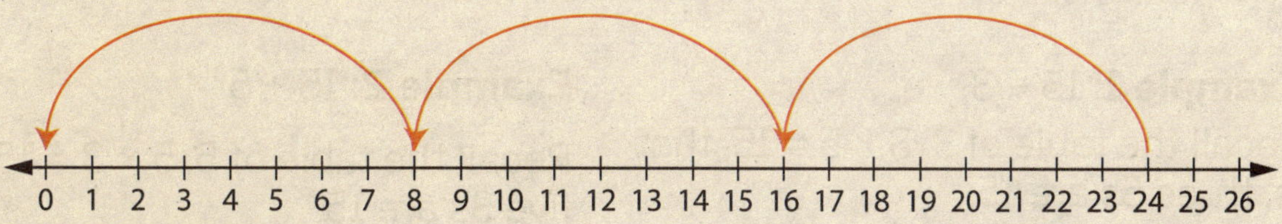

Division Fact = ______________

(b)

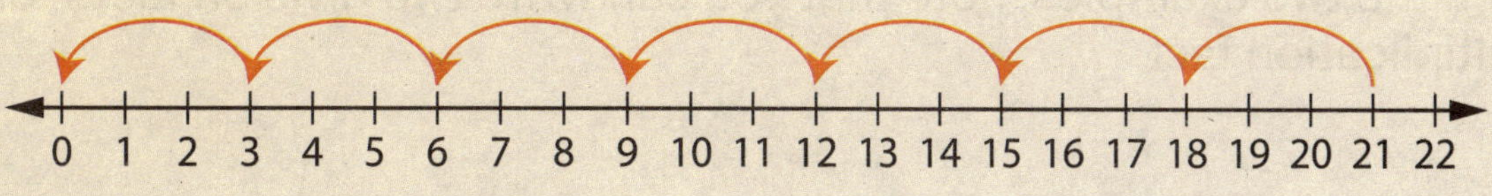

Division Fact = ______________

RELATION BETWEEN MULTIPLICATION AND DIVISION

There are 4 balloons in a bunch. How many balloons will there be in 3 such bunches?

4 + 4 + 4 = 12, so there will be a total of 12 balloons.

It can also be written as 3 × 4 = 12. → Multiplication Fact

Consider the same problem in a different way. If there are 12 balloons and 4 balloons are in one bunch, then how many such bunches will be there?

12 divided by 4 gives 3. That is, 12 ÷ 4 = 3. → Division Fact

Now, observe both multiplication and division facts together.

4 × 3 = 12 12 ÷ 4 = 3

Note that multiplication is the opposite of division. Also, division is the opposite of multiplication.

Therefore, multiplication tables can be used to understand division.

Example 1: 15 ÷ 3

Recall the table of 3. 3 × 5 = 15, that is, three 5s are 15.

Therefore, 15 ÷ 3 = 5.

Example 2: 15 ÷ 5

Recall the table of 5. 5 × 3 = 15, that is, five 3s are 15.

Therefore, 15 ÷ 5 = 3.

From the two examples, note that you can write two division facts for a given multiplication fact.

3 × 5 = 15

→ Division Fact 1: 15 ÷ 3 = 5

→ Division Fact 2: 15 ÷ 5 = 3

Exercise 1.4

1 **Write the multiplication facts for the following division problems. The first one has been done for you.**

(a) $10 \div 5 = 2$ [$2 \times 5 = 10$] and [$5 \times 2 = 10$]

(b) $18 \div 9 = 2$ [ ] and [ ]

(c) $36 \div 6 = 6$ [ ] and [ ]

(d) $48 \div 8 =$ ____ [ ] and [ ]

(e) $20 \div 5 =$ ____ [ ] and [ ]

2 **Use the multiplication tables and solve the division problems.**

(a) $6 \div 2 =$ ____ (b) $40 \div 5 =$ ____ (c) $14 \div 7 =$ ____

(d) $21 \div 3 =$ ____ (e) $25 \div 5 =$ ____ (f) $30 \div 10 =$ ____

(g) $27 \div 9 =$ ____ (h) $63 \div 9 =$ ____ (i) $72 \div 8 =$ ____

(j) $16 \div 2 =$ ____ (k) $28 \div 4 =$ ____ (l) $15 \div 3 =$ ____

(m) $18 \div 2 =$ ____ (n) $24 \div 4 =$ ____ (o) $50 \div 5 =$ ____

TERMS USED IN DIVISION

The number 12 divided by 4 gives 3.

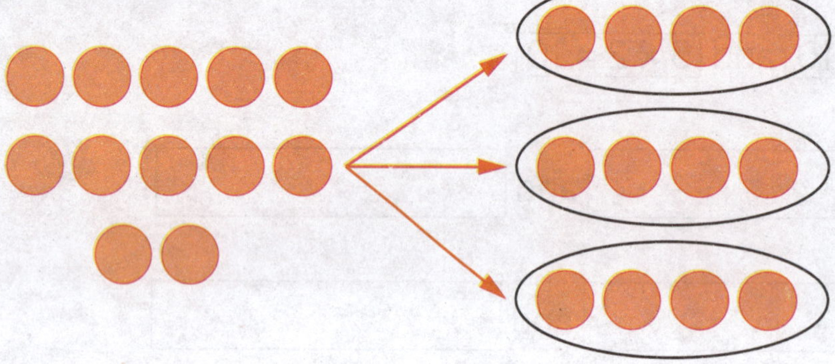

$12 \div 4 = 3$

Each number in the division fact has a name as shown below.

Divisor ↖ $12 \div 4 = 3$ ↗ **Quotient**

↓ **Dividend**

Dividend: The number which is divided is the dividend. In other words, it is the total number of objects to be distributed.

Divisor: The number which divides is called the divisor. In other words, it is equal to the number of objects in each equal group.

Quotient: The result of the division is called the quotient. In other words, it is equal to the number of equal groups.

Example 1: In $14 \div 2 = 7$, 14 is the dividend, 2 is the divisor and 7 is the quotient.

Example 2: In a division problem, Dividend = 56, Divisor = 7 and Quotient = 8.

Write the division fact in the form of Dividend ÷ Divisor = Quotient.

The division fact for the above division problem is $56 \div 7 = 8$.

Dividend ÷ Divisor = Quotient

Exercise 1.5

1 Identify the dividend, divisor and quotient and fill in the blanks in the following division problems.

(a) 27 ÷ 9 = 3 Dividend = _____ Divisor = _____ Quotient = _____

(b) 24 ÷ 4 = 6 Dividend = _____ Divisor = _____ Quotient = _____

(c) 30 ÷ 3 = _____ Dividend = _____ Divisor = _____ Quotient = _____

2 Write the division fact for each of the following division problems.

(a) Dividend = 16 Divisor = 8 Quotient = 2 ____ ÷ ____ = ____

(b) Dividend = 30 Divisor = 5 Quotient = 6 ____ ÷ ____ = ____

(c) Dividend = 81 Divisor = 9 Quotient = ____ ____ ÷ ____ = ____

PROPERTIES OF DIVISION

Division of a Number by Itself

Three bananas are to be shared equally among 3 children. How many bananas will each one get?

Each one gets 1 banana. That is, 3 ÷ 3 = 1.

Observe the following division facts and fill in the blanks.

2 ÷ 2 = 1	5 ÷ 5 = 1	8 ÷ 8 = 1	10 ÷ 10 = ____
4 ÷ 4 = 1	6 ÷ 6 = ____	7 ÷ 7 = ____	7 ÷ 7 = ____

A number divided by itself is equal to 1.

Division of a Number by 1

Consider the example, if there are 5 balloons and all the balloons are given to only one child, then the child gets all the 5 balloons. This can be written as 5 ÷ 1 = 5.

Observe the following division facts and fill in the blanks.

2 ÷ 1 = 2	3 ÷ 1 = 3	4 ÷ 1 = 4	10 ÷ 1 = ___
5 ÷ 1 = 5	6 ÷ 1 = ___	9 ÷ 1 = ___	8 ÷ 1 = ___

A number divided by 1 is equal to the number itself.

Division of 0 by a Number other than Zero

There are two kids. But, there are no fruits to be shared between them. This means that they get no fruits. In other words, they get 0 fruits. So, it can be written as 0 ÷ 2 = 0.

0 divided by any number, other than zero, is equal to 0.

Note: A number divided by zero is not defined.

Exercise 1.6

1 Solve the following problems.

(a) 8 ÷ 8 = _____ (b) 12 ÷ 1 = _____ (c) 0 ÷ 2 = _____

(d) 50 ÷ 50 = _____ (e) 0 ÷ 39 = _____ (f) 25 ÷ 1 = _____

WORD PROBLEMS

Example: The cost of 7 ice creams is ₹56. Find the cost of one ice cream.

Cost of 7 ice creams = ₹56.

Therefore, cost of 1 ice cream = 56 ÷ 7 = 8

Hence, one ice cream costs ₹8.

Verification: Quotient × Divisor = Dividend

8 × 7 = 56

Exercise 1.7

Solve the following word problems.

1. Three chocolates cost ₹15. Find the cost of one chocolate.

2. If 8 bus tickets cost ₹32, then what will be the cost of each ticket?

3. If there are 64 spoons in 4 packets, then how many spoons are there in each packet?

4. 63 bulbs are placed in 7 boxes, how many bulbs are there in each box?

Revision Exercise

1 **Write the division facts and their answers.**

(a) Share 36 sweets equally among 6 students.

(b) There are 40 pencils. A box can hold 5 pencils. How many boxes are needed to put all pencils?

2 **Recall the multiplication tables and complete the following division facts.**

(a) $12 \div 4 =$ _____ (b) $10 \div 2 =$ _____ (c) $50 \div 10 =$ _____

(d) $24 \div 6 =$ _____ (e) $21 \div 3 =$ _____ (f) $90 \div 9 =$ _____

3 **Solve the following division facts using repeated subtraction.**

(a) $9 \div 3 =$ _____ (b) $15 \div 5 =$ _____ (c) $18 \div 3 =$ _____

(d) $14 \div 7 =$ _____ (e) $36 \div 9 =$ _____ (f) $63 \div 7 =$ _____

4 **Write the multiplication facts for the following division facts. One has been done for you.**

(a) $16 \div 8 =$ 2	8 × 2 = 16 ;	2 × 8 = 16
(b) $63 \div 7 =$ _____	_____ × _____ = _____ ;	_____ × _____ = _____
(c) $8 \div 2 =$ _____	_____ × _____ = _____ ;	_____ × _____ = _____

5 **There are 24 plants equally planted in 4 rows. Find the number of plants in each row.**

6 **81 notebooks are to be distributed equally among 9 students. How many notebooks will each one get?**

INTRODUCTION TO LONG DIVISION

12 ÷ 4 = 3

Let us represent this division using the long division method.

```
             3  ← Quotient
Divisor → 4)12  ← Dividend
           -12
             0  ← Remainder
```

Identify the division terms in the following and write them in the blanks.

Divison is yet another operation of mathematics.
It needs a **Dividend** and a **Divisor**.
The **Dividend** gets divided.
The **Divisor** divides dividend.
The **Quotient** is the answer.
And what remains is the **Remainder!**

(1)

```
              9  ← ______
______ → 3)27  ← ______
            -27
              0  ← ______
```

(2)

```
              8  ← ______
______ → 5)40  ← ______
            -40
              0  ← ______
```

Complete the table given below.

Divison	Dividend	Divisor	Quotient	Remainder
35 ÷ 7 7)35 = 5, −35, 0	35			0
18 ÷ 2		2		
28 ÷ 4				
72 ÷ 9				

WORKSHEET

Divide the following items into equal groups. Circle the equal groups and write the division facts. One has been done for you.

1. Make equal groups of 4. 24 ÷ 4 = 6

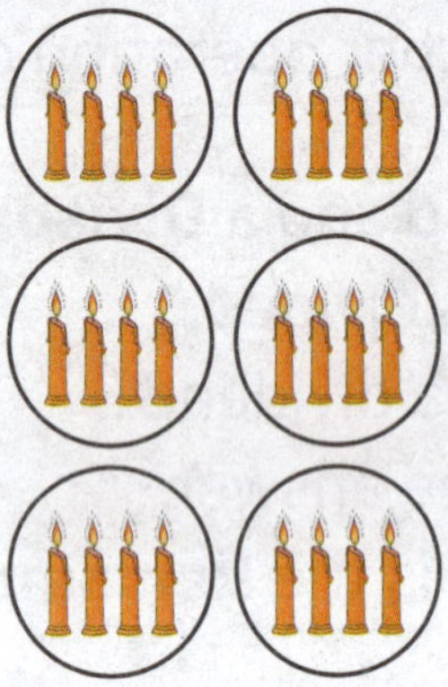

2. Make equal groups of 7. _____ ÷ _____ = _____

3. Make equal groups of 2. _____ ÷ _____ = _____

4. Make equal groups of 5. _____ ÷ _____ = _____

HOTS (Higher Order Thinking Skill)

Sonam is thinking of a number that can be made into groups of 2 completely. It can also be made into groups of 5 completely. What is that number?

2 Measurements

Learning Objectives

- To express length in centimetres and metres
- To express weight in grams and kilograms
- To express capacity in millilitres and litres

Let's Get Started

Pick the correct words from the clouds and fill in the blanks.

longer shorter

The monkey's tail is _____ than the dog's tail.

lighter heavier

The zebra is _____ than the cat and the cat is _____ than the zebra.

more less

The bucket holds _____ water than the tub. The tub holds _____ water than the bucket.

MEASUREMENT OF LENGTH

A handspan, a cubit and a pace can be used for measuring the lengths of objects.

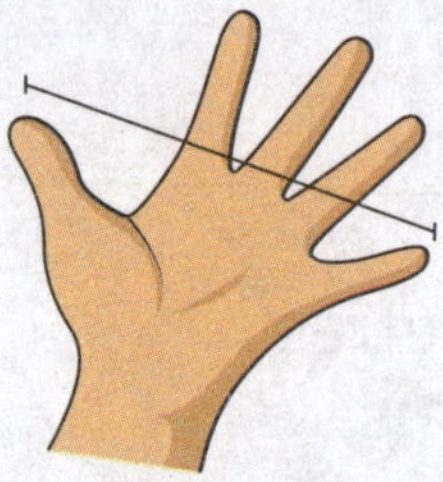

Handspan

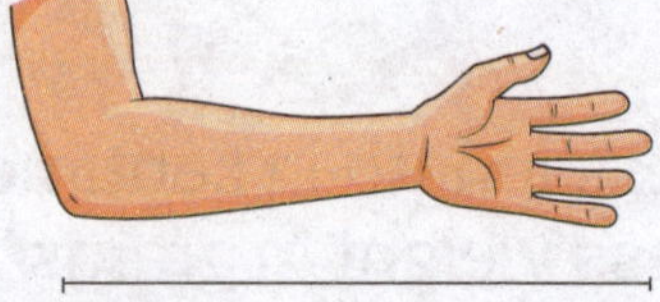

Cubit

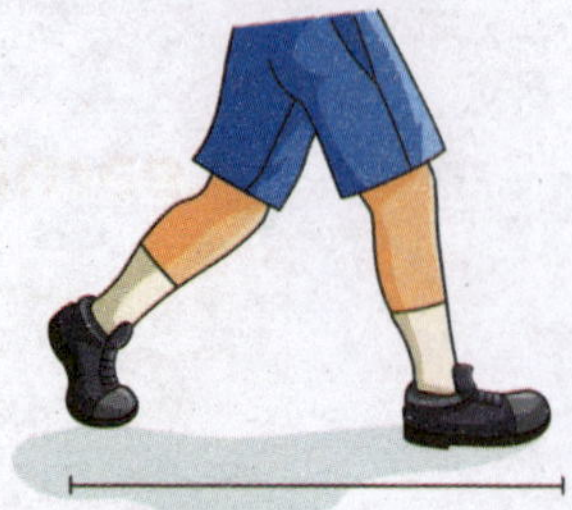

Pace

These are the non-standard units of measurement.

You and your teacher measure the lengths of the following in handspan, cubit and pace:

1. The length of one side of this textbook (in handspan)
2. The side of the table (in cubit)
3. The length of the classroom (in pace)

The measurements taken by you and your teacher would differ. This is because different people have different lengths for handspan, cubit and pace. That is why we need standard units of measurements.

Units of Length

The standard unit of length is **metre**. One metre is divided into 100 smaller units called **centimetre**.

The units 'metre' and 'centimetre' are used to measure short distances and the lengths of different objects. Metre is written as 'm' and centimetre is written as 'cm'. The length of the ruler used in the geometry box is 15 cm.

1 m = 100 cm

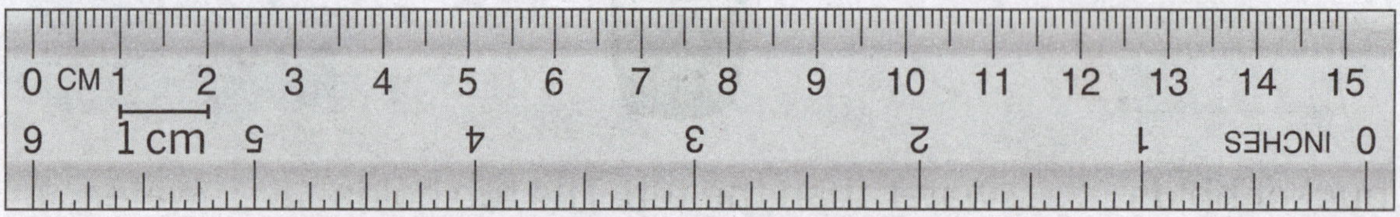

The unit 'centimetre' is used to measure the lengths and widths of small objects.

Note: The word 'about' is used to show that the measurements are not exact.

A sharpener measures about 2 cm.

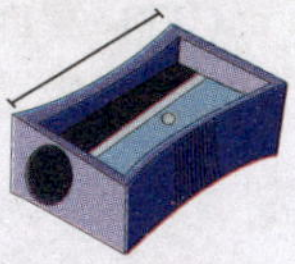

Your forefinger measures about 3 cm.

The thickness of this book is about 1 cm.

The unit 'metre' is used to measure the lengths and widths of bigger objects and shorter distances.

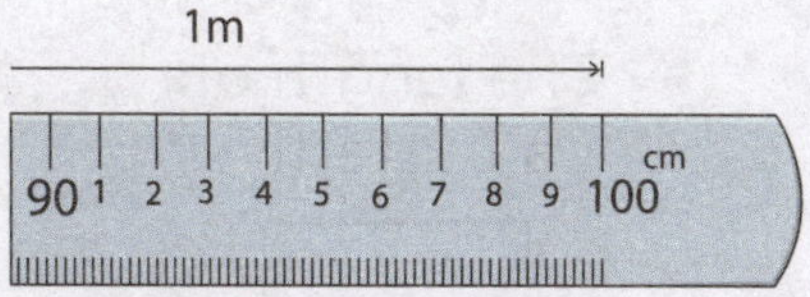

The length of your classroom is about 10 m.

The length of a saree is about 6 m.

Given below are some tools used for measuring length.

Measuring tape

Metre stick

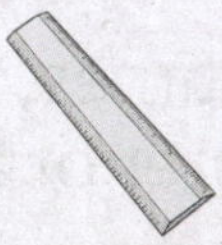

Ruler

Do You Know!

The world's smallest fish measures about the same length as the nail on your little finger.

Example: Choose the correct unit of measurement for measuring the lengths of the objects given alongside.

cm ✓m 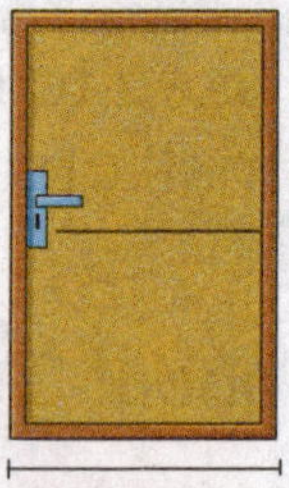 ✓cm m 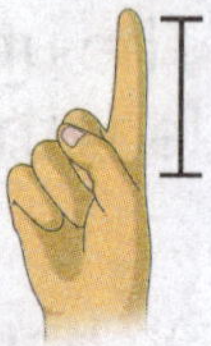

Exercise 2.1

1 **Choose the correct units and write them in the boxes given.**

cm m

The length of a butterfly

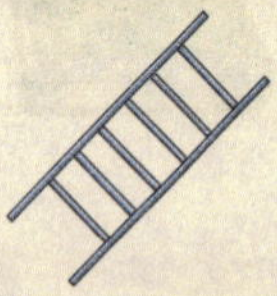

The height of a ladder

The length of a door curtain

The length of your nose

2 **Fill in the blanks with cm or m.**

(a) The length of a door is 3 _____.

(b) The length of a notebook is 15 _____.

(c) The length of a nail is 5 _____.

(d) The length of a playground is 100 _____.

MEASUREMENT OF MASS (WEIGHT)

You know that a heavier object weighs more than a lighter object.

Sometimes, it is difficult to say which is heavier or lighter of the two objects.

Which is lighter: your ruler or your pencil?

Which is heavier: your water bottle or your lunch box?

So, suitable units are required to measure the mass of objects.

Rock

Pebble

The rock is heavier than the pebble and the pebble is lighter than the rock.

Units of Mass

1 kg = 1000 g

The standard unit of mass is **gram**. 1000 grams make a **kilogram**.

The unit 'gram' is used to measure weights of lighter objects. The unit 'kilogram' is used to measure weights of heavier objects. Gram is written as 'g' and kilogram is written as 'kg'.

Objects such as a pencil, an eraser or a sharpener weigh a few grams.

Pencil

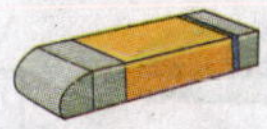
Eraser

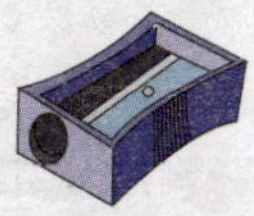
Sharpener

Objects such as a school bag, a chair or a table weigh a few kilograms.

An eraser weighs about 20 g.

A school bag weighs about 4 kg.

A stool weighs about 15 kg.

School bag

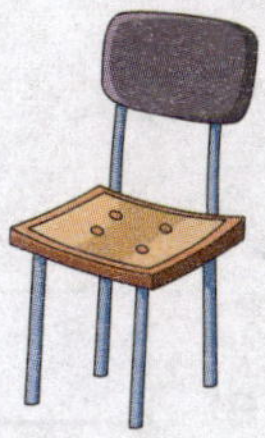
Chair

Table

Physical Balance

A physical balance is an instrument used to measure weight.

Parts of a Physical Balance

When two objects of same masses are kept in each of the two pans of a physical balance, the pans are balanced and stay at the same level. But when the masses of the objects in the pans are not same, the pan with the heavier object goes down and the pan with the lighter object goes up.

Physical Balance

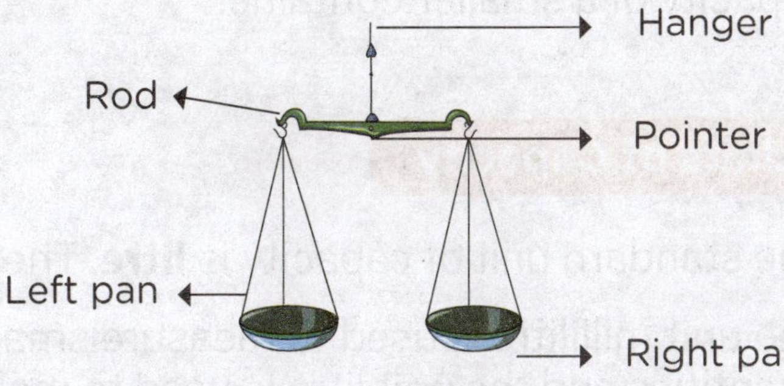

Exercise 2.2

Choose the correct units of weight and write them in the boxes given.

g kg

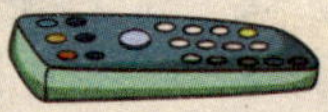

TV remote ☐

Table ☐

TV ☐

Fruit basket ☐

Marble ☐

Football ☐

CAPACITY (VOLUME)

The amount of liquid that a container can hold is called its **capacity**.

The capacity of a bigger container is more than the capacity of a smaller container.

Cup

Glass

Which container holds more: the cup or the glass?

Units of Capacity

The standard unit of capacity is **litre**. There are 1000 **millilitres** in one litre.

The unit millilitre is used to measure smaller quantities and the unit litre is used to measure the capacities of bigger containers.

$1\ \ell = 1000\ m\ell$

Litre is written as 'ℓ' and millilitre is written as '$m\ell$'.

Litre is used to measure the capacities of a bucket, a tank, a pool, etc.

Millilitre is used to measure the capacities of a spoon, a cup, a glass, etc.

Spoon Cup Glass

A spoon contains about 5 mℓ of syrup.

A glass contains about 100 mℓ of milk.

A tank contains about 100 ℓ of water.

Different tools called 'measuring jars' are used to measure the capacities. Some measuring jars have mℓ or ℓ marked on them.

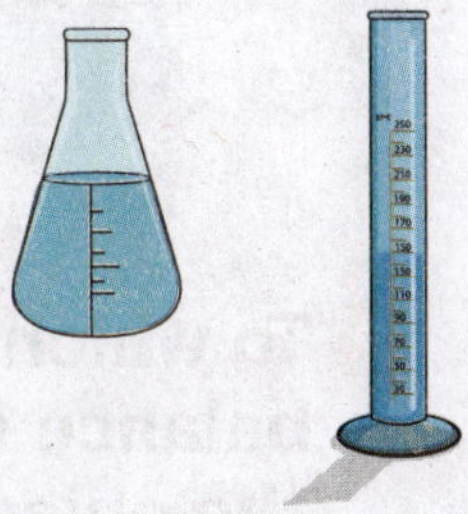

Which container among the bucket, jug and glass will you use to fill the oil tank shown?

It will be easier to fill the oil tank with the bucket.

Exercise 2.3

1 Choose the correct units of capacity and write them in the boxes given.

ℓ mℓ

 ☐  ☐  ☐  ☐

Revision Exercise

1 Circle the correct tool that you will use to measure in each case given below. One has been done for you.

(a) The length of this glass

(b) The weight of this bag

(c) The capacity of this fish bowl

(d) The length of this mirror

2 To which pan should the objects given below go to make the balance of pans as shown below. Write R in the box given under the object that goes into the right pan and write L in the box given under object that goes into the left pan. One has been done for you.

(a)

(b)

(c)

3 Write *more* or *less* to show that the container has more than 1 litre or less than 1 litre liquid.

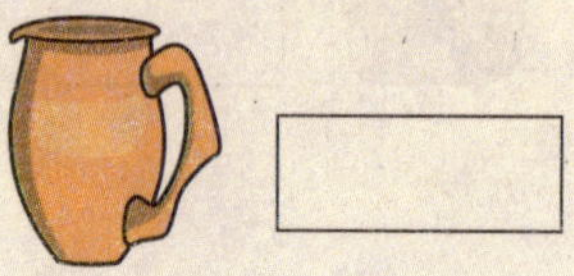

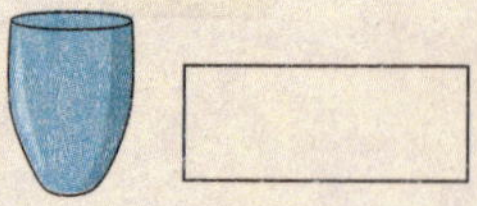

Maths Lab Activity

Aim: To arrange the containers in an order based on their volumes

Materials required:

- Water
- A marker
- 5 different containers such as glass, mug, jug, bottle, small tub
- A 5-litre transparent tub that has markings on it for measurement

Procedure:

1. Have the students work in groups.
2. Ask them to take all the containers and guess which holds more/less water.
3. Ask them to arrange them in order, container holding most water to least water.
4. Now, ask them to check their guesses by following the steps given below.
   (a) Mark the five containers as A, B, C, D and E.
   (b) Fill container A with water.
   (c) Pour the water of container A into the transparent tub. Mark the water level as A and pour back the water.
   (d) Note down the water level.
   (e) Repeat the same process with containers B, C, D and E.
   (f) Order the five containers A, B, C, D and E on the basis of your measurements.
5. Ask the students to check if their guesses were correct.

HOTS (Higher Order Thinking Skill)

Some children are playing on the seesaw in the park. They want to know who balances whom on the seesaw. Sunny is sitting on the left side of the seesaw. Name the children who will have to sit on the right side of the seesaw to balance Sunny.

Sunny weighs 30 kg

Ram weighs 15 kg

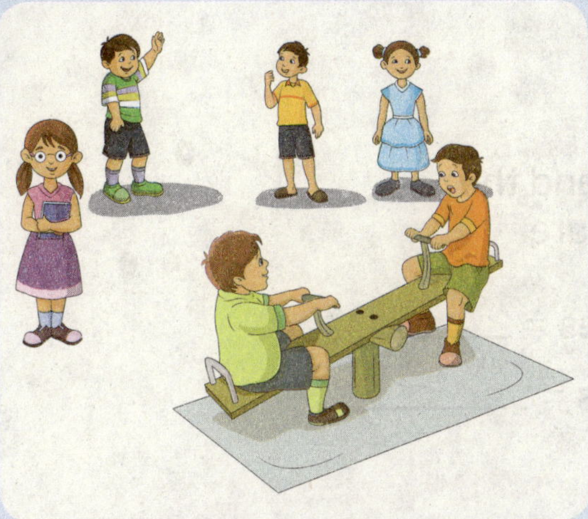

Nayan weighs 12 kg

Ann weighs 8 kg

Sita weighs 10 kg

3 Shapes and Patterns

Learning Objectives

- To identify objects that roll and objects that slide
- To identify the corners and sides of a given flat shape
- To recognize different number patterns

Let's Get Started

Match the following pictures with the types of lines used to create them.

Straight lines only

Curved lines only

Straight lines + Curved lines

We are straight lines.

We are curved lines.

Join the straight lines and the curved lines in the picture.

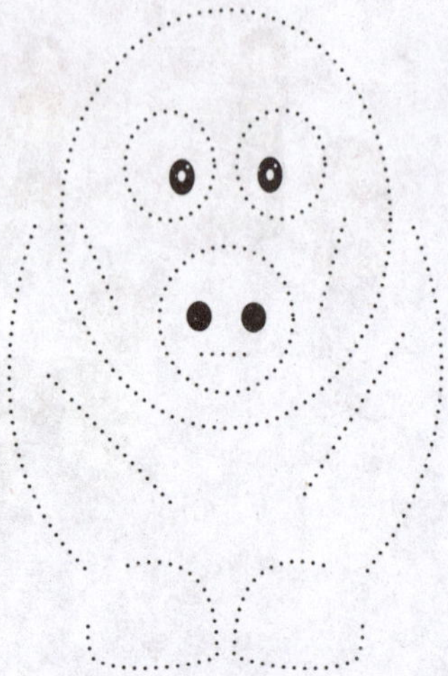

Number of straight lines = ________

Number of curved lines = ________

SOLID OBJECTS

Look at the objects that you see in and around your home.

All these objects are **solid shapes**.

ROLLING AND SLIDING

Look at the following pictures.

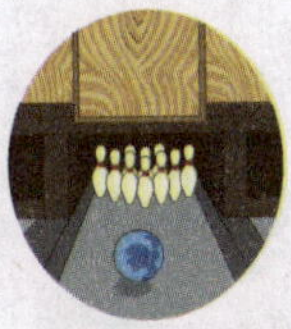

In all the above pictures, the objects are **rolling**.
Some of the objects which can roll are shown below.

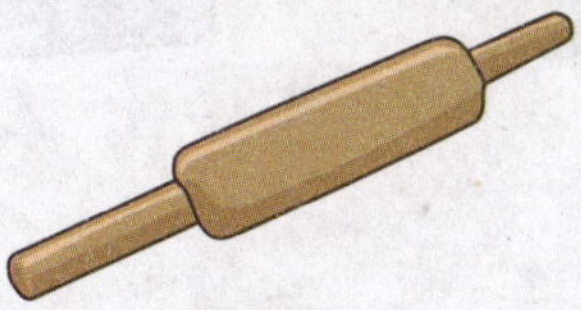

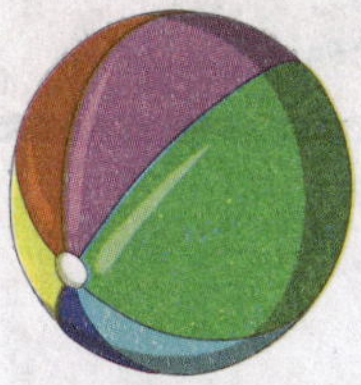

Look at the following pictures.

In all the above pictures, people are **sliding**.
Some of the objects which can slide are shown below.

Exercise 3.1

Match the objects with the suitable text boxes given below by drawing lines.

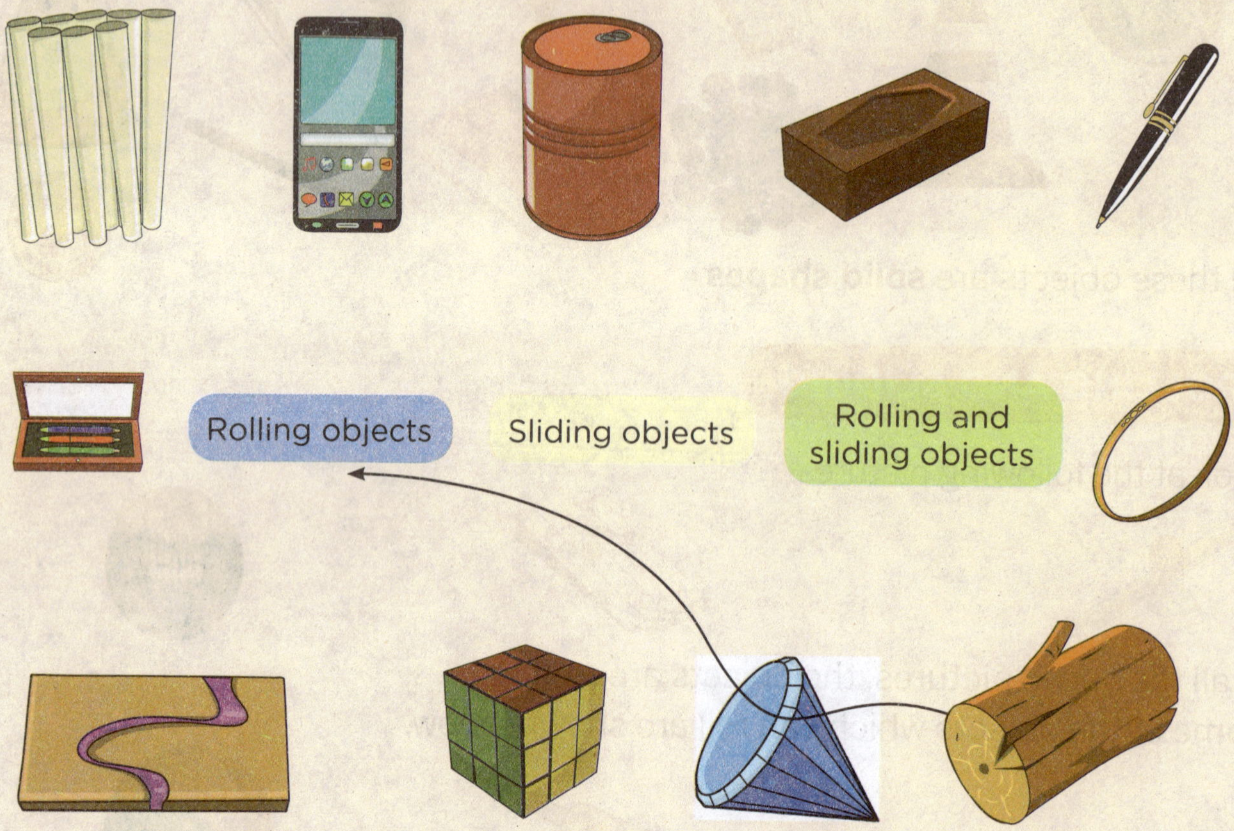

Look at the following objects. They can both **roll** and **slide**.

FLAT AND SOLID SHAPES

Write the names of the shapes given below. One has been done for you.

Circle				

Shapes like circle, square, recangle, triangle and oval are known as **flat** or **plane shapes**.

Exercise 3.2

Match the objects given below to their shapes given in the box in the centre.

These shapes are known as **solid shapes**. Look at the names of these solid shapes.

Cube	Cuboid	Cylinder	Cone	Sphere

Exercise 3.3

Write the names of the solid shapes of the objects given below. A few have been done for you.

Sphere

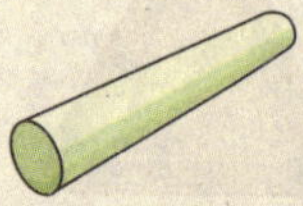
Cylinder

Cuboid

Cube

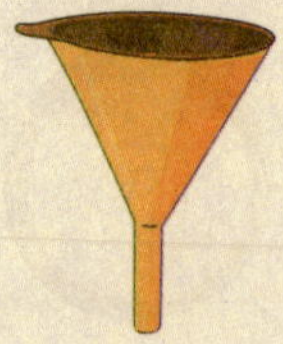
Cone

____

____

____

____

____

____

____

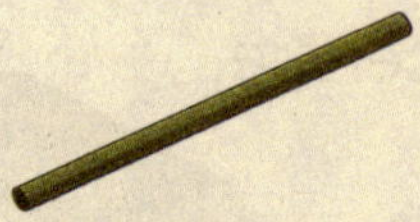
____

CORNERS AND EDGES

Look at the following plane shapes.

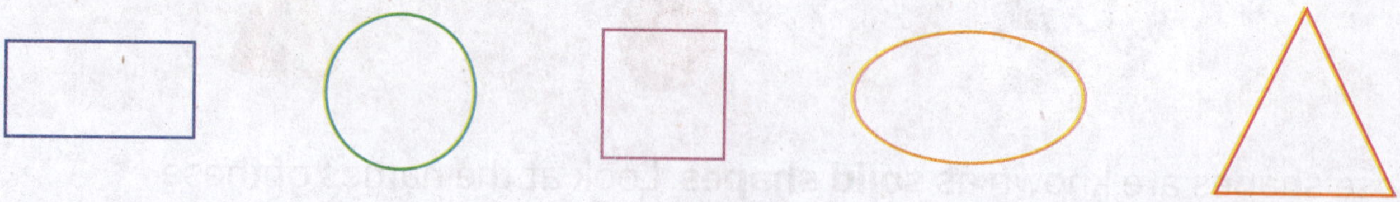

Each shape is made by either curved lines or straight lines. These lines are known as **edges** or **sides**.

Observe that these figures (rectangle, square and triangle) have straight lines as their edges. Hence they are known as **straight edges**.

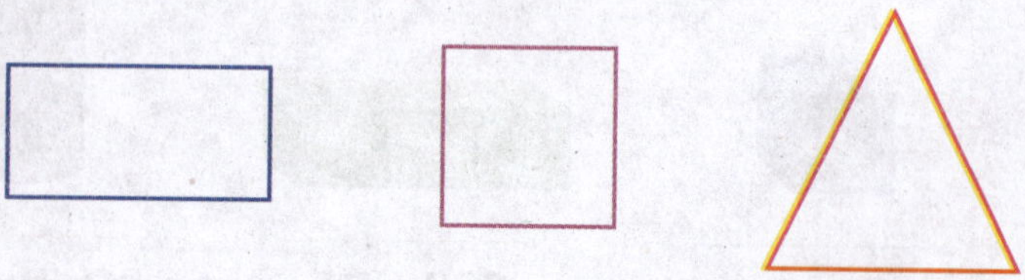

Look at some objects with straight edges or sides.

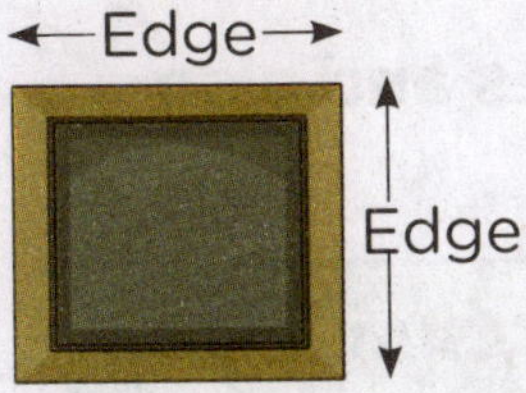

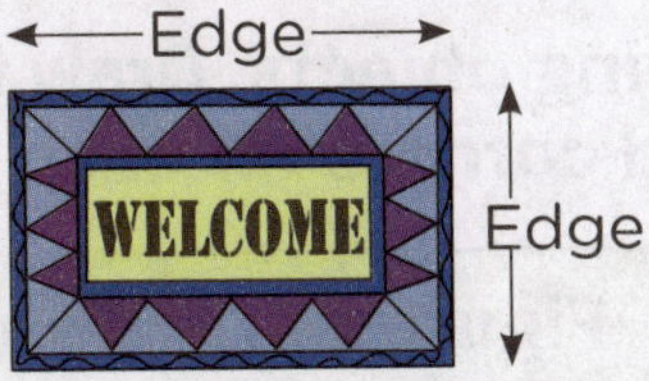

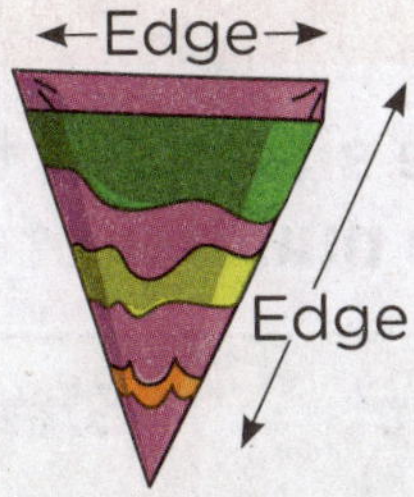

The points where the edges meet are known as **corners**.

Observe that these figures (circle and oval) have curved lines as their edges. Hence they are known as **curved edges** or sides.

Look at some objects with curved edges or sides.

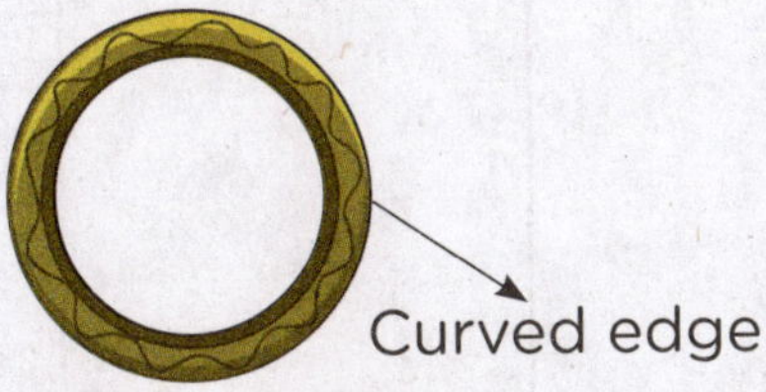

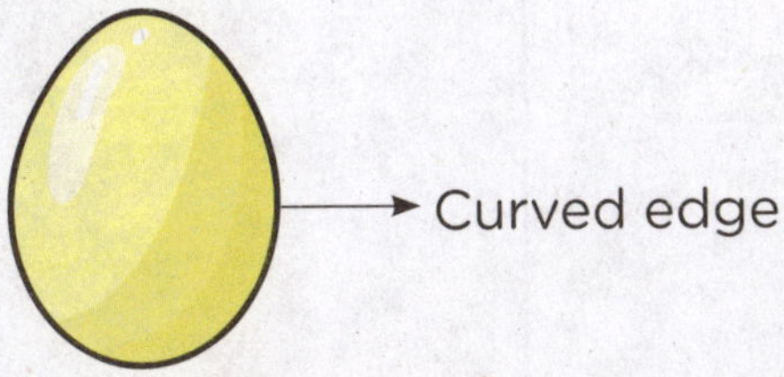

Rectangle

A rectangle has 4 straight edges and 4 corners.

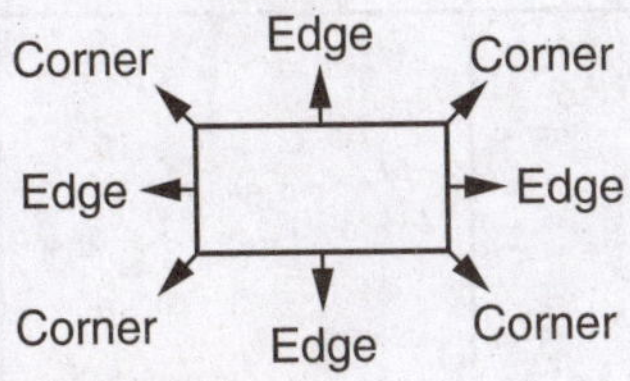

Square

A square has 4 straight edges and 4 corners.

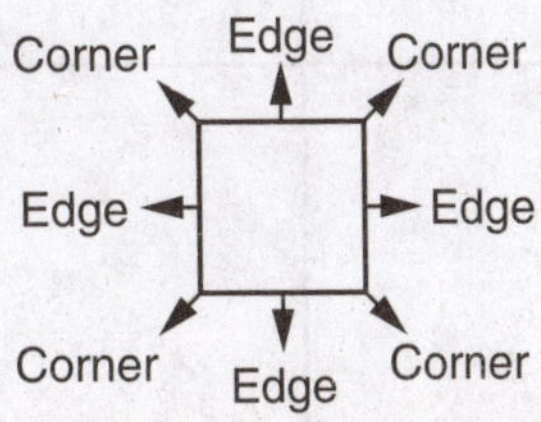

Triangle

A triangle has 3 straight edges and 3 corners.

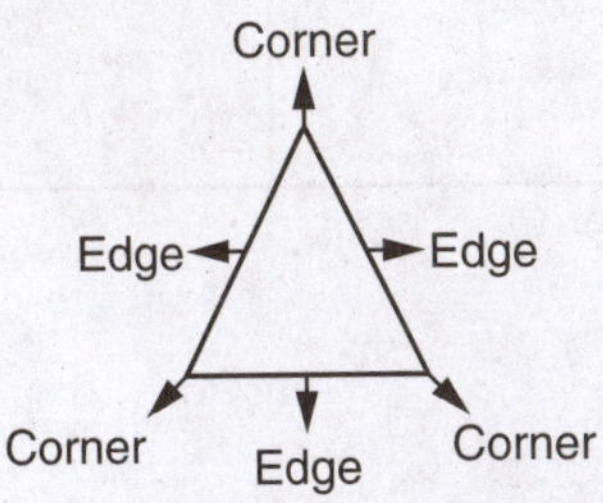

Circle and Oval

Circle and oval have one curved edge and no corners.

Exercise 3.4

Write the shapes of the following objects. Draw the shapes and also write the number of edges and corners for each object.

Object	Shape	Figure	Number of Edges	Number of Corners
	Square		4	4

PATTERNS

What will come next?

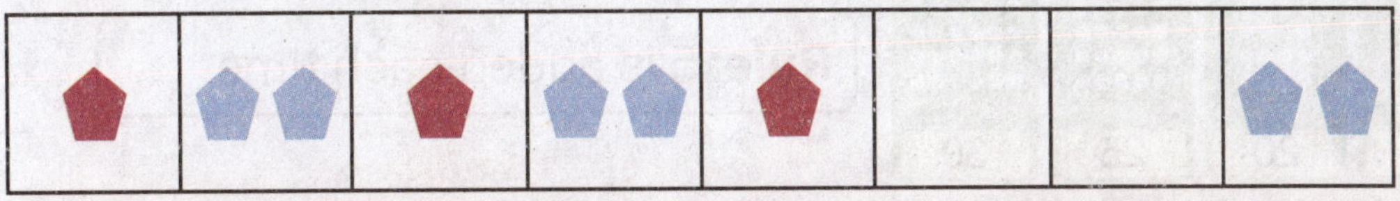

Exercise 3.5

1 Colour the pictures to complete the pattern.

(a)

(b)

2 Draw the missing shapes in the patterns.

(a)

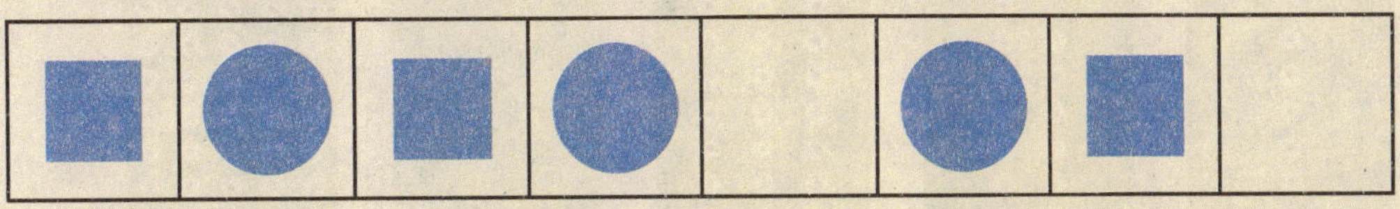

(b)

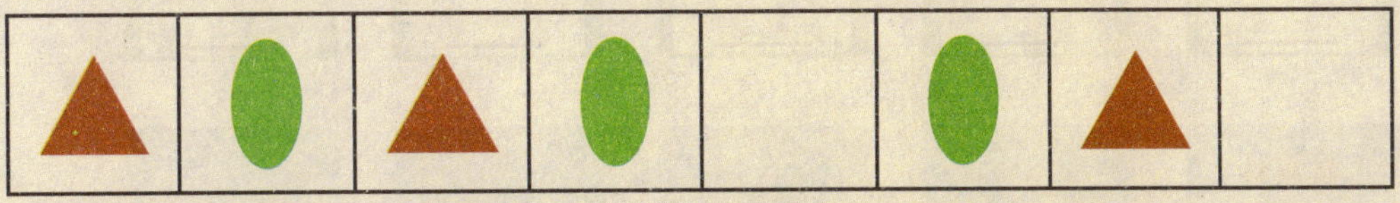

3 Create your own pattern by using the given shapes.

Observe the following patterns of numbers.

Rule: 2 is added each time.

Rule: 5 is added each time.

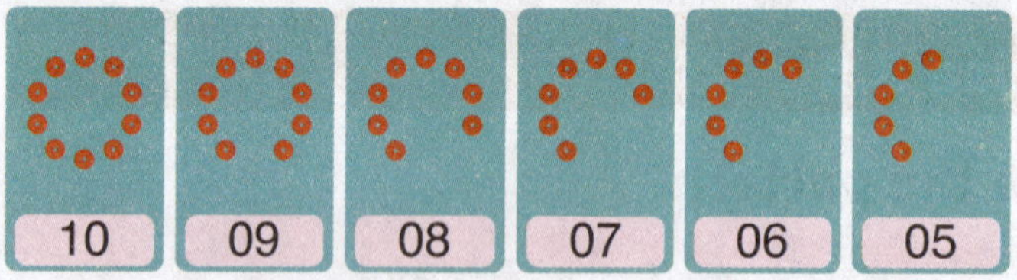

Rule: 1 is subtracted each time.

Exercise 3.6

Count and write the number of objects in each box. Also, complete the pattern.

(a)

(b)

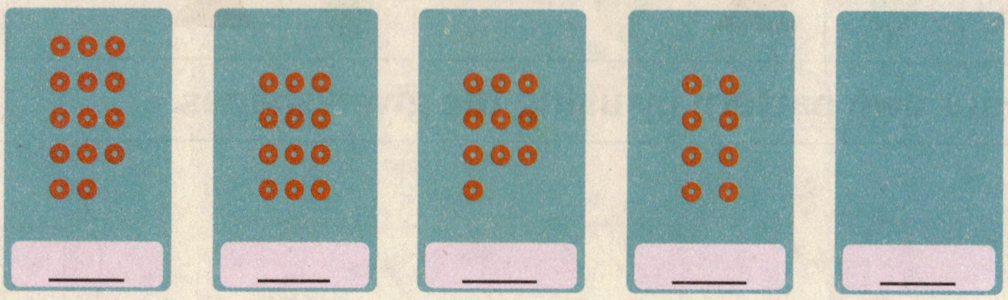

Revision Exercise

1 For the following objects, write (R) if the object rolls, (S) if it slides or (R and S) if the object both rolls and slides.

(a) 

(b) 

(c) 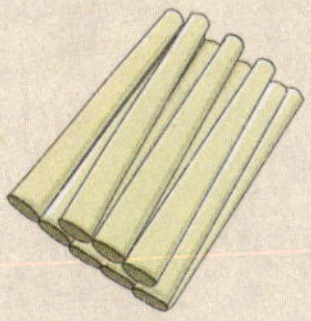

2 Match the solids with their names.

Cube	Cuboid	Cylinder	Cone	Sphere

3 Identify the corners and edges of the following pictures. Also specify whether the edges are straight or curved.

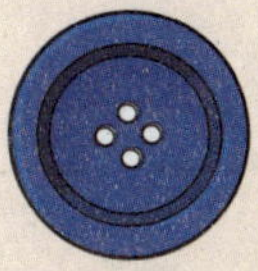

Edges: ______ (Straight/Curved)

Corners: ______

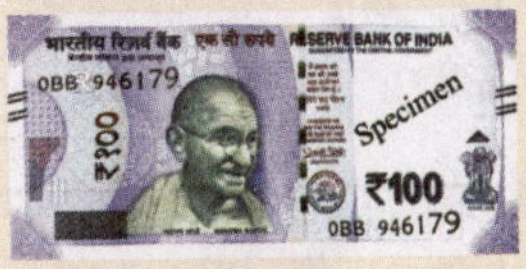

Edges: ______ (Straight/Curved)

Corners: ______

Edges: ______ (Straight/Curved)

Corners: ______

Edges: ______ (Straight/Curved)

Corners: ______

Maths Lab Activity

Aim: To classify objects into rolling, sliding and rolling as well as sliding objects

Materials required: Different objects as shown:

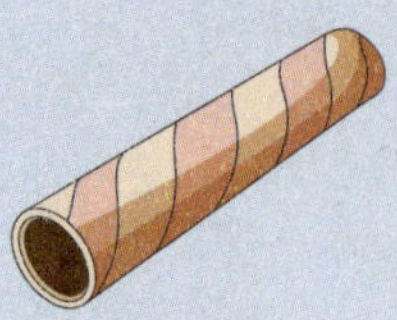
Tube

Plate

Paper weight

Pen stand

Box
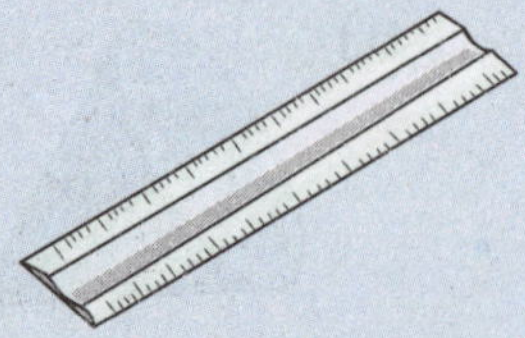
Scale

Coin

Marble
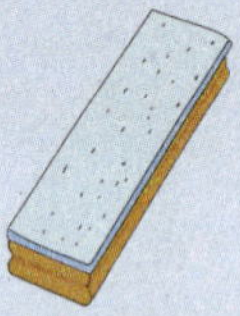
Duster

Beads
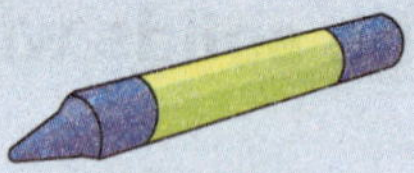
Crayon

Funnel

Procedure:

1. Make an inclined surface using a book on the table.
2. Place the objects one by one on the book.
3. Observe whether the object rolls, slides or rolls as well as slides.
4. Complete the table given below for any five objects by drawing them.

Object	Rolling (R)/Sliding (S)/Sliding & Rolling (R & S)

ASSESSMENT 1

Chapters 1-3

A Choose the correct option for each of the following.

1. The concept of sharing equally is known as
   (a) addition (b) division (c) subtraction (d) multiplication
2. If 12 ice creams are distributed equally among 6 students, how many will each get?
   (a) 1 (b) 3 (c) 2 (d) 4
3. How many boxes are required to pack 50 mugs if each box can hold 10 mugs?
   (a) 5 (b) 10 (c) 50 (d) 2
4. 42 ÷ 7 =
   (a) 5 (b) 7 (c) 24 (d) 6
5. Which of the following will be measured in metre?
   (a)  (b)  (c)  (d) 
6. Which of the following is the correct way of writing 250 millilitres?
   (a) 250 (b) 250 m (c) 250 mℓ (d) 25 mls
7. Which unit will you use to measure the weight of a water balloon?
   (a) Gram (b) Millilitre
   (c) Kilogram (d) Litre

8. Which amongst the following is not a solid shape?
   (a)  (b)  (c)  (d) 
9. Which of the following objects both roll and slide?
   (a)  (b)  (c)  (d) 
10. Identify the object which does not have curved edges.
   (a)  (b)  (c)  (d) 

B Fill in the blanks.

1. There are 48 plants in 8 rows. The number of plants in each row is ________ .
2. If 85 is divided by 9, the quotient will be ________ .
3. The amount of liquid that a container holds is called its ________ .
4. 1 kg = ________ g
5. A triangle has ________ corners and ________ straight edges.

C State whether the following statements are true (T) or false (F).

1. In the division fact 27 ÷ 9 = 3, the divisor is 3. ☐
2. A number divided by 1 is equal to the number itself. ☐
3. The repeated subtraction facts for 14 ÷ 7 = 2 is 14 − 2 = 12, 12 − 2 = 10, 10 − 2 = 8, 8 − 2 = 6, 6 − 2 = 4, 4 − 2 = 2, 2 − 2 = 0. ☐
4. A figure can be made up of both curved lines and straight lines. ☐
5. A glass of milk has about 20 ℓ of milk in it. ☐

D Match the following.

Column A

Weight of a jug

Length of a jug

Column B

Measured in centimetre

Measured in gram

4 Money

Learning Objectives

- To make different combinations of rupees and coins for the given amounts
- To add and subtract different amounts

Let's Get Started

We need money to buy things. In India, the currency used for money is Rupee. Notes and coins of different values are used.

Some of the notes and coins used in India are:

Write two different combinations using the same coins to make ₹10. One has been done for you.

(a)

			(₹5 + ₹2 + ₹3) ₹10
1 (₹5)	1 (₹2)	3 (₹3)	

(b)

			__________ ₹10

ADDITION OF MONEY

- Mrs Rao visited her brother's family for Deepawali. She bought 2 gifts for each of her 2 nieces and 3 nephews.

The cost of all the gifts is given below.

₹10

₹83

₹90

₹48

₹40

₹75

₹27

₹15

₹56

Note: The symbol '₹' is used for 'Rs' and 'Re'.

Let us find out how much she spent for each child.

(a) Ruma's gifts are the handbag and the perfume bottle.

Cost of Ruma's gifts = 83 + 48 = ______

₹83

₹48

$$\begin{array}{r} 83 \\ +\ 48 \\ \hline ₹\ 131 \\ \hline \end{array}$$

(b) Rajesh's gifts are the belt and the pen set.

Cost of Rajesh's gifts = 75 + 90 = ______

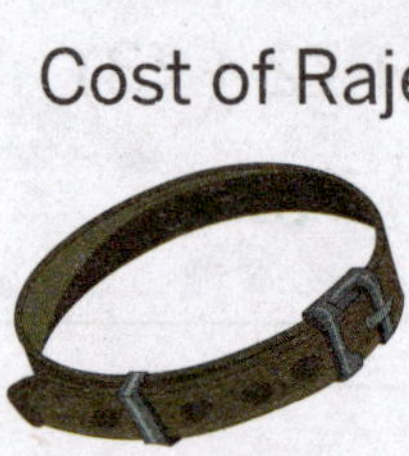
₹75

₹90

$$\begin{array}{r} 75 \\ +\ 90 \\ \hline ₹\ 165 \\ \hline \end{array}$$

(c) Rahul's gifts are storybook and the pencil box.
Cost of Rahul's gifts = 27 + 56 = ______

₹27

₹56

```
   2 7
 + 5 6
₹ ____
```

(d) Roopa's gifts are the doll and a chocolate.
Cost of Roopa's gifts = 40 + ______ = ______

₹40

₹10

```
   4 0
 +
₹ ____
```

(e) Ravi's gifts are a chocolate and a box of crayons.
Cost of Ravi's gifts = 10 + ______ = ______

₹10

₹15

```
   1 0
 +
₹ ____
```

To add the amounts, always start from the biggest amount.

Exercise 4.1

1 **Find the sum of the prices of each pair of objects on the left side and match the combination of notes and coins on the right side by drawing lines.**

 ₹32 ₹20	
 ₹10 ₹50	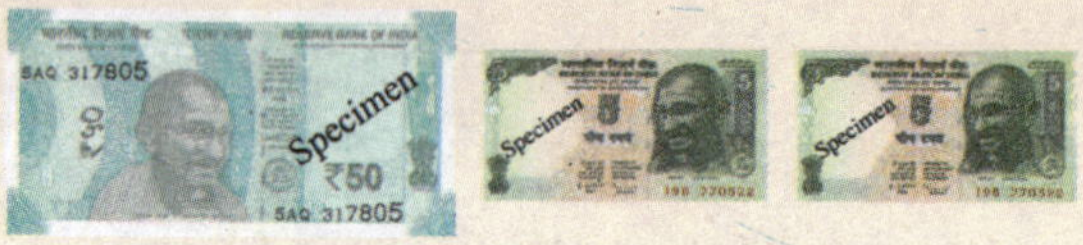
 ₹65 ₹14	

2 **Shilpa bought the following items from a grocery store. How much did she pay to the shopkeeper?**

₹5

₹28

₹60

₹55

Sum of the items she bought =

₹_____ + ₹_____ + ₹_____ + ₹_____ = ₹________

Shilpa paid ₹________ to the shopkeeper.

3 **Vivek has ₹50. Name the two items he can buy from the stationery shop.**

Gel Pen (blue)	₹15
Ball Pen (blue)	₹10
Ball Pen (black)	₹10
Sketch Pen Set	₹35
Chart Paper (white)	₹12

Vivek can buy ____________

and ____________ for ₹50.

Cost of item 1 = ₹____________

Cost of item 2 = ₹____________

Total cost = ₹____________

SUBTRACTION OF MONEY

At the theatre, Anuradha and her brother Mihir got ₹50 each to spend on eatables. Anuradha bought a packet of popcorn for ₹35 and Mihir bought a sandwich for ₹28. How much money is remaining with each of them?

- Anuradha spent ₹35.

  Amount remaining with her = ₹50 – ₹35 = ₹________

$$\begin{array}{r} 5\,0 \\ -\,3\,5 \\ \hline ₹\;1\,5 \\ \hline \end{array}$$

Anuradha has ₹15 left with her.

- Mihir spent ₹28.

  Amount remaining with him = ₹50 – ₹28 = ₹________

$$\begin{array}{r} 5\,0 \\ -\,2\,8 \\ \hline ₹\;2\,2 \\ \hline \end{array}$$

Mihir has ₹22 left with him.

- Mihir wants to eat popcorn also, how much more money does he need?

  Cost of the popcorn = ₹35

  Amount Mihir has = ₹22

  Amount Mihir needs = ₹35 – ₹22 = ₹________

  Mihir needs ₹________ more.

$$\begin{array}{r} 3\,5 \\ -\;\;\;\; \\ \hline ₹\;\;\;\; \\ \hline \end{array}$$

Exercise 4.2

1 **Match the following by drawing lines.**

Item bought and amount paid	Amount returned
	₹2
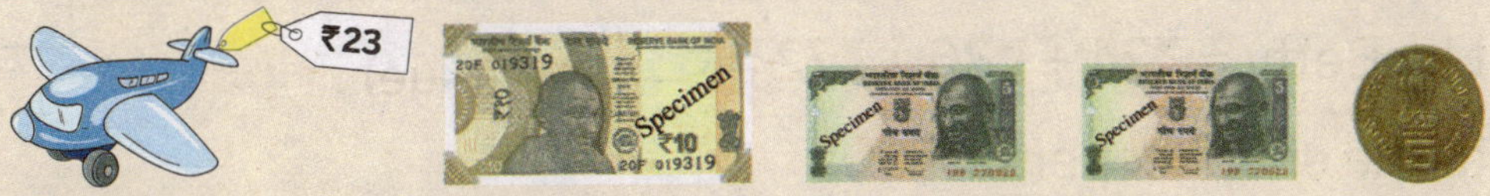	₹3
	₹15

2 **Amit wants to buy one dozen marbles. They cost ₹42. He has ₹35 with him. How much more does he need to buy the marbles?**

Cost of the marbles = ₹__________

Amount Amit has = ₹__________

The difference in amount needed to buy the marbles

= ________ – ________ = ₹________

3 **Latheef has ₹77 in his wallet. How much more money does he need to make it ₹100?**

Amount Latheef has = ₹________

Amount he wants to make = ₹________

Amount required = ₹________ – ₹________ = ₹________

ADDITION AND SUBTRACTION OF MONEY

(a) Aseem gave a ₹50 note and a ₹10 note to pay ₹52 for the vegetables he bought from a grocery shop. How much did the shopkeeper return?

Amount Aseem paid = ₹50 + ₹10 = ₹60

Cost of the vegetables = ₹52

Amount returned by the shopkeeper = ₹60 – ₹52 = ₹8

(b) Betty bought rice flour for ₹24, wheat flour for ₹36 and some *daal* for ₹72. She paid ₹150 to the shopkeeper. What was the amount she spent and how much did she get back?

$$\begin{array}{r} 24 \\ +\ 36 \\ +\ 72 \\ \hline 132 \\ \hline \end{array}$$

Amount spent by Betty = ₹24 + ₹36 + ₹72 = ₹__________

Amount paid to the shopkeeper = ₹150

$$\begin{array}{r} 150 \\ -\ 132 \\ \hline 18 \\ \hline \end{array}$$

Amount returned by the shopkeeper = ₹150 – ₹132 = ₹__________

Betty paid ₹132 and got back ₹18.

Exercise 4.3

Thapar's shop sells boxes of different kinds.

₹101 ₹110 ₹75 ₹99 ₹164

1. Diya bought a box of cost ₹75 and another of cost ₹164. She gave Thapar 2 notes of ₹100 and a note of ₹50. How much did she spend and how much did she get back?

   Amount spent by Diya = ₹75 + ₹164 = ₹________

   $$\begin{array}{r} 75 \\ +\ 164 \\ \hline \\ \hline \end{array}$$

   Amount paid by Diya = ₹100 + ₹100 + ₹50 = ₹________

   Amount she got back = ₹250 − ₹________ = ₹________

   $$\begin{array}{r} 250 \\ - \quad \\ \hline \\ \hline \end{array}$$

   Diya bought boxes for ₹________ and got back ₹________.

2. Tina wants to buy 2 boxes for her friends. She has a total of ₹200 with her. Which 2 boxes can she buy if the shopkeeper returns ₹15 to her?

   Total amount that Tina has = ₹________

   Amount the shopkeeper returns to her = ₹________

   Thus, amount she spent = ₹________ − ₹________ = ₹________

   Two boxes Tina bought are ₹________ + ₹________ = ₹185.

Revision Exercise

1 State whether the following statements are true (T) or false (F).

(a) 3 notes of ₹10 make ₹30. ☐

(b) A note of ₹50 is more than 5 notes of ₹10. ☐

(c) 2 coins of ₹2 and 3 coins of ₹1 make ₹5. ☐

2 Circle the correct notes and coins to make the amount given.

₹35 

3 Sateesh has 1 note of ₹50, 2 notes of ₹20, 2 coins of ₹5 and 2 coins of ₹2. How much money does he have in all?

(a) ₹72 (b) ₹102 (c) ₹92 (d) ₹104

4 Deepa went to a shop and bought the following items. She gave ₹100 to the shopkeeper. How much money did she get back?

Maths Lab Activity

Aim: To find the various combinations for ₹50

Materials required: Sets of play money

Procedure:

1. Make the students work in groups.
2. Each group should have the following notes.
   - 2 notes of ₹20 • 2 notes of ₹10 • 3 coins of ₹5 • 5 coins of ₹2 • 5 coins of ₹1

3. Find five different combinations to make ₹50.
4. Write your combinations in a table.

5 Time

Learning Objectives

- To read time to half past an hour
- To identify days of the week and months of the year

Let's Get Started

1. Fill in the missing numbers on the face of the clock.

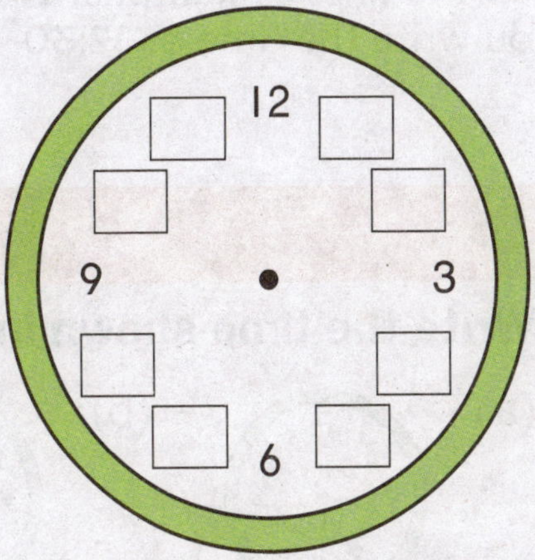

2. Draw the minute hand and the hour hand to show the time written below.

11:00

2:00

6:00

READING TIME TO HALF PAST THE HOUR

The minute hand takes one hour to go around the clock. The hour hand in the same time goes from one number to the next. The minute hand moves faster than the hour hand.

When the minute hand starts from 12 and reaches 6, then the time is half past an hour.

The minute hand is on 6.
The hour hand is between 12 and 1.
You read the time as **half past twelve**.
You write the time as **12:30**.

The minute hand is on 6.
The hour hand is between 4 and 5.
You read the time as **half past four**.
You write the time as **4:30**.

Exercise 5.1

1 **Write the time shown in the clocks below.**

(a)  ____________

(b)  ____________

(c)  ____________

(d)  ____________

2 **Draw the hour hand on the clocks to show the given time. The minute hand is already drawn.**

(a) 1:30 

(b) 9:30 

(c) 11:30 

(d) 4:30 

3 **Given below is Rohan's timetable for Sunday. Fill in the blanks by looking at the clocks in the pictures.**

(a) Rohan wakes up at __________.

(b) Rohan takes bath at __________.

(c) Rohan helps his mom in the kitchen at __________.

(d) Rohan and his family have breakfast at __________.

(e) Rohan takes his pet to the vet at __________.

(f) Rohan returns home with the pet at __________.

DAYS OF THE WEEK

There are seven days in a week. The days of the week in the correct order are shown in the following table.

1	2	3	4	5	6	7
Monday	Tuesday	Wednesday	Thursday	Friday	Saturday	Sunday
First (1st)	Second (2nd)	Third (3rd)	Fourth (4th)	Fifth (5th)	Sixth (6th)	Seventh (7th)

Which day of the week do you like the most? ____________________

Which is the third day of the week? ____________________

Which is the fifth day of the week? ____________________

MONTHS OF THE YEAR

There are 12 months in a year.

First	January
Second	February
Third	March
Fourth	April
Fifth	May
Sixth	June
Seventh	July
Eighth	August
Ninth	September
Tenth	October
Eleventh	November
Twelfth	December

Exercise 5.2

1 Given below is Purva's timetable for the week.

Monday	Tuesday	Wednesday	Thursday	Friday	Saturday	Sunday
Piano	Dance	Karate	Yoga	No classes	Music	Chess

Now answer the following questions.

(a) On which day does Purva go for the music class? ____________

(b) On which day does Purva go for the karate class? ____________

(c) On which day does Purva go for the chess class? ____________

(d) On which day does Purva have no classes? ____________

2 Match the following.

Column A	Column B
The week begins on	Tuesday
This day that comes after Thursday	Thursday
This day comes before Wednesday	Sunday
This day falls before Thursday	Monday
This day falls between Wednesday and Friday	Friday
This day falls between Friday and Sunday	Wednesday
The last day of the week	Saturday

3 **Look at the calendar below and then answer the questions that follow.**

2018

January

S	M	T	W	T	F	S
	1	2	3	4	5	6
7	8	9	10	11	12	13
14	15	16	17	18	19	20
21	22	23	24	25	26	27
28	29	30	31			

February

S	M	T	W	T	F	S
				1	2	3
4	5	6	7	8	9	10
11	12	13	14	15	16	17
18	19	20	21	22	23	24
25	26	27	28			

March

S	M	T	W	T	F	S
				1	2	3
4	5	6	7	8	9	10
11	12	13	14	15	16	17
18	19	20	21	22	23	24
25	26	27	28	29	30	31

April

S	M	T	W	T	F	S
1	2	3	4	5	6	7
8	9	10	11	12	13	14
15	16	17	18	19	20	21
22	23	24	25	26	27	28
29	30					

May

S	M	T	W	T	F	S
		1	2	3	4	5
6	7	8	9	10	11	12
13	14	15	16	17	18	19
20	21	22	23	24	25	26
27	28	29	30	31		

June

S	M	T	W	T	F	S
					1	2
3	4	5	6	7	8	9
10	11	12	13	14	15	16
17	18	19	20	21	22	23
24	25	26	27	28	29	30

July

S	M	T	W	T	F	S
1	2	3	4	5	6	7
8	9	10	11	12	13	14
15	16	17	18	19	20	21
22	23	24	25	26	27	28
29	30	31				

August

S	M	T	W	T	F	S
			1	2	3	4
5	6	7	8	9	10	11
12	13	14	15	16	17	18
19	20	21	22	23	24	25
26	27	28	29	30	31	

September

S	M	T	W	T	F	S
						1
2	3	4	5	6	7	8
9	10	11	12	13	14	15
16	17	18	19	20	21	22
23	24	25	26	27	28	29
30						

October

S	M	T	W	T	F	S
	1	2	3	4	5	6
7	8	9	10	11	12	13
14	15	16	17	18	19	20
21	22	23	24	25	26	27
28	29	30	31			

November

S	M	T	W	T	F	S
				1	2	3
4	5	6	7	8	9	10
11	12	13	14	15	16	17
18	19	20	21	22	23	24
25	26	27	28	29	30	

December

S	M	T	W	T	F	S
						1
2	3	4	5	6	7	8
9	10	11	12	13	14	15
16	17	18	19	20	21	22
23	24	25	26	27	28	29
30	31					

(a) Name the month that comes before December. ____________

(b) Name the month that comes before March. ____________

(c) How many Fridays are there in November? ____________

(d) Which day is 6th January? ____________

(e) Complete the table.

Months which have 30 days	Months which have more than 30 days

Dates on consecutive weekdays

Look at 3 consecutive Saturdays of any month. Let us say, the first 3 Saturdays of May.

May 2018

Sunday	Monday	Tuesday	Wednesday	Thursday	Friday	Saturday
		1	2	3	4	5
6	7	8	9	10	11	12
13	14	15	16	17	18	19
20	21	22	23	24	25	26
27	28	29	30	31		

The dates are 5, 12 and 19. What is the difference between 2 consecutive Saturdays?

$12 - 5 = 7$ $19 - 12 = 7$

The difference between two consecutive Mondays or two consecutive Tuesdays or any other consecutive weekdays is always 7.

If you know the date of a weekday, you can find the date of that day next week by adding 7 or of that day the previous week by subtracting 7.

If today is Monday, 13th, what was the date on last Monday and what will be the date on next Monday?

Knuckle Trick

Shortcut to remember the number of days in every month:

Starting with your forefinger's knuckle

1st knuckle: January – 31 days

Groove: February – 28 or 29 days

2nd knuckle: March – 31 days

Groove: April – 30 days

3rd knuckle: May – 31 days

Groove: June – 30 days

4th knuckle: July – 31 days

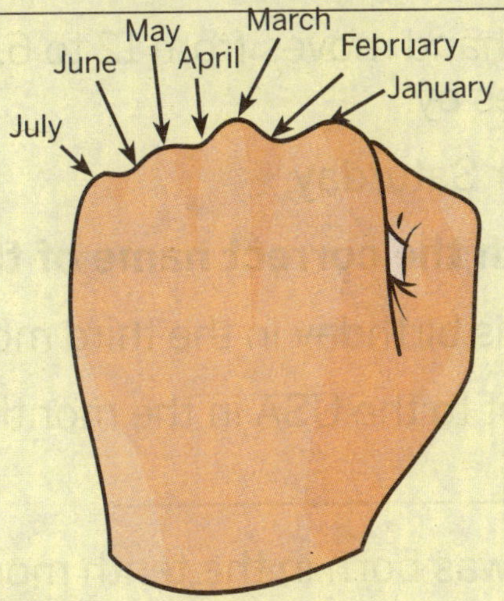

Returning to your forefinger's knuckle

1st knuckle: August – 31 days

Groove: September – 30 days

2nd knuckle: October – 31 days

Groove: November – 30 days

3rd knuckle: December – 31 days

Revision Exercise

1 Write the time shown in each of the clocks below.

(a)  ________

(b)  ________

(c)  ________

(d)  ________

2 Fill in the boxes.

If Today is [ ]

Tomorrow will be [ ]

Yesterday was [ ]

Day after tomorrow will be [ ]

Day before yesterday was [ ]

3 Read the sentences and mark (✓) or (✗).

(a) Two days after Tuesday is Wednesday. ☐

(b) Sunday is the last day of the week. ☐

(c) February always has 29 days. ☐

(d) When the minute hand moves from 12 to 6, then half an hour passes by. ☐

(e) Friday comes after Saturday. ☐

4 Fill in the blanks with the correct name of the month.

(a) Anup celebrates his birthday in the third month. ________

(b) Maya's father went to the USA in the month having the least number of days. ________

(c) Mahatma Gandhi was born in the tenth month. ________

Maths Lab Activity

Aim: To identify the months of a year

Materials required:
Placards with all the 12 months written — 3 sets, that is, $3 \times 12 = 36$ placards

Procedure:

1. Have 3 sets (so that all students can participate at the same time) of placards ready with the name of each month written on each placard.
2. Give one placard to each child.
3. Students to hold the placards with both their hands in front of them.
4. Ask each complete group to stand in a horizontal line in the correct order from January to December.
5. All the students to read out aloud the names of the months in order.

6. Now have them stand in a circle. Play music or clap hands and students should go around in the circle.
7. Stop clapping or playing the music and call out the name of any month by giving a hint. For example, the month that comes after May, the shortest month, etc.
8. All those students who have the placard of that month's name should raise their placards above their heads.
9. After 3 rounds, call out multiple months. For example, the first and the last month, the months that begin with the letter 'J', the last three months, etc.
10. After 3 rounds, now when the music stops, ask the students to stand in a line in the correct order from January to December.

HOTS (Higher Order Thinking Skills)

Write the following.

(a) The number of weeks in a year ____________

(b) The number of days in a year ____________

(c) The number of weeks in a leap year ____________

(d) The number of days in a leap year ____________

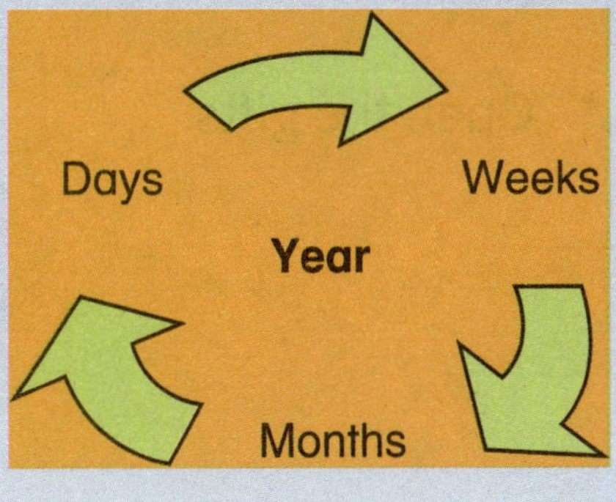

WORKSHEET

WORKSHEET

It's Ryan's birthday next Sunday!

Ryan is happy as he has been allowed to plan his birthday party.

Given below are the things to be done. Help Ryan plan by filling these in the table given below. Two have been done for you.

- Prepare the guest list 
- Send invitations 

- Order birthday cake 
- Clean up the place 
- Decorate the place 
- Prepare the menu 
- Open the gifts 

Weekday	Things to do
Monday	
Tuesday	
Wednesday	
Thursday	Order birthday cake
Friday	
Saturday	
Sunday	Birthday party; Open the gifts

6 Data Handling

Learning Objective

- To make a list of items

Let's Get Started

Banwari has some animals in his farm. He counts them every day when they come back from the forest. Look at his list and check if all the animals have come back.

List of animals

Horse – 1	Goats – 2	Cows – 3
Rooster – 1	Sheep – 2	Hen – 4

MAKING A LIST

1. Aanya is playing with her building blocks. Before she puts them away, she checks with her list to see if every block is there.

List of blocks
Red – 4
Pink – 4
Blue – 6
Yellow – 4
Orange – 4

Making a list helps you to organize your tasks and makes it easier to work with things.

Look at her list. Has she missed out something?

2. There are different kinds of trees in an orchard.

Let us make a list of all the trees.

Coconut trees – 8
Mango trees – 4
Banana trees – 3
Papaya trees – 6

(a) How many different types of trees are there in the orchard?

There are 4 different types of trees.

(b) How many more coconut trees are there than papaya trees?

There are 2 more coconut trees than papaya trees.

(c) The number of mango trees is more than the number of papaya trees. (True/False) False

(d) What is the total number of trees in the orchard?

There are 21 trees in the orchard.

Revision Exercise

1 **Rajat's friends are coming to his house in the evening. His mother cooked a variety of dishes. Complete the list of food items and answer the questions given below.**

(a) How many varieties of food items has Rajat's mother prepared?

____

(b) How many more burgers are there than sandwiches?

____

(c) Among *samosa* and burgers, which is less in number?

____

2 **Given below are the favourite sweets of 16 children.**

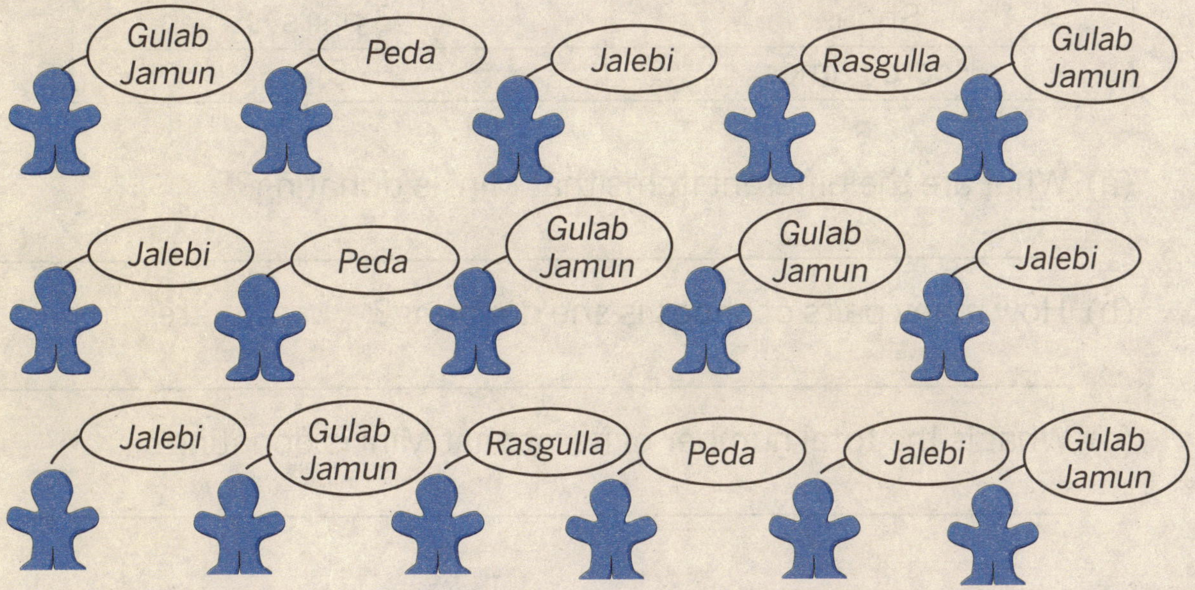

Complete the list and answer the questions given below.

Name of the Sweet	Number of Children
Gulab Jamun	6
Peda	
Jalebi	
Rasgulla	2

(a) Which sweet is liked by most of the children?

____

(b) Which sweet is liked by the least number of children?

____

(c) The number of children who like *Peda* is more than the number of children who like *Jalebi*. (True/False) _______________

3 **Mini has made a list of the things to donate.**

Name of the Item	Number of Items
Toys	10
Storybooks	15
Dresses	8
Shoes	3 pairs
Board games	5

(a) What are the different items that Mini is donating?

____

(b) How many pairs of shoes is she donating?

____

(c) What is the total number of items that Mini is donating?

____

Maths Lab Activity

Aim: To make a list of words

Procedure:

1. Divide your class into groups.
2. Write down the word DICTIONARY in your notebook.
3. Make as many 2-letter, 3-letter and 4-letter words as possible using the letters in the word 'DICTIONARY', without repeating letters in a word (for example, air, rat, road, etc). Write your words in the following box.

2-letter words:

3-letter words:

4-letter words:

4. Count the words made by your group and complete the list.

Words	Number of Words
2-letter words	
3-letter words	
4-letter words	
Total	

5. Answer the following questions based on the table above.
   (a) How many words could you make in all?
   ____
   (b) Which letter words are the least in number? How many?
   ____
   (c) Which letter words are the most in number? How many?
   ____
   (d) The number of 2-letter words is more than the number of 4-letter words. (True/False)
   ____
   (e) Can you write a 5-letter or a 6-letter word?
   ____

WORKSHEET

WORKSHEET

Colour the stars given below in different colours. Use the colours red, blue, yellow and green. Then complete the list.

Colour of the Star	Number of Stars

7 Introduction to Fractions

Learning Objective

- To understand fraction of a region and the terms 'numerator' and 'denominator'

Let's Get Started

There is one whole cake. 

Divide the whole cake into two equal parts.

Divide the whole cake into three equal parts.

Divide the whole cake into four equal parts.

Each part is one-half.

Each part is one-third.

Each part is one-fourth.

These are fractions of one.

When an object or a group of things is divided into **equal parts**, then each part is a fraction of the whole.

Part of a Whole

When the whole object is one, it is called a region.

Fraction *means* **part of a whole**.

A **whole** can either be a region or a collection.

When there is a group of objects, it is called a collection.

Example: Look at the given figure. This is a whole pizza.

This pizza can be cut into parts.

Example: This is a whole collection of mangoes.

We can take a part of this collection by taking 4 mangoes.

FRACTION OF A REGION

Example 1:

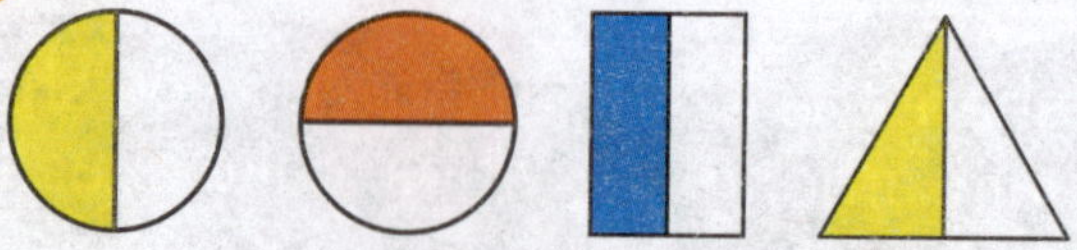

Look at the figures.

Each shape is divided into 2 equal parts. One part is shaded in each shape.

Each shaded part of the shape is **one-half of the whole**. It is written as $\frac{1}{2}$.

That is, $\dfrac{\textit{Number of shaded parts}}{\textit{Total number of parts in a whole}} = \dfrac{1}{2}$

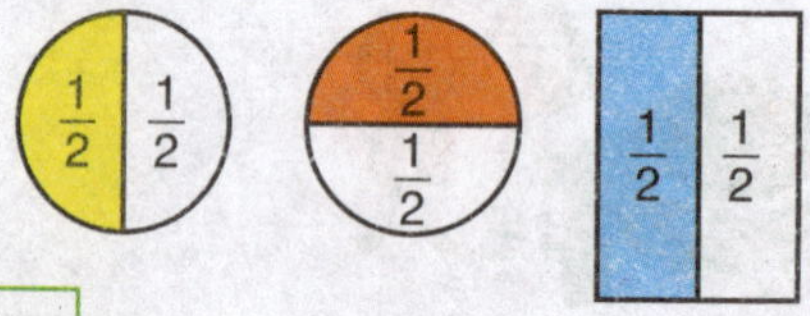

Example 2:

Each shape is divided into 3 equal parts. One out of the 3 parts is shaded.

Each shaded part of the shape is **one-third of the whole**. It is written as $\frac{1}{3}$.

That is, $\dfrac{\textit{Number of shaded parts}}{\textit{Total number of parts in a whole}} = \dfrac{1}{3}$

Example 3:

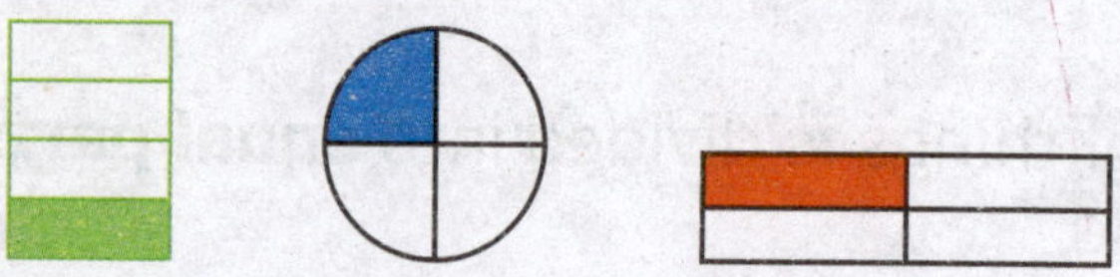

Each shape is divided into 4 equal parts. One out of the 4 parts is shaded. Each shaded part of the shape is **one-fourth of the whole**. It is written as $\frac{1}{4}$.

That is, $\dfrac{\textit{Number of shaded parts}}{\textit{Total number of parts in a whole}} = \dfrac{1}{4}$

NUMERATOR AND DENOMINATOR

Look at this figure.

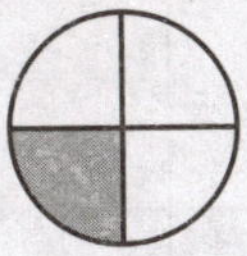

It is written as $\frac{1}{4} = \dfrac{\text{Numerator}}{\text{Denominator}}$

Numerator → It shows the number of equal parts which have been shaded.

Denominator → It shows the number of equal parts into which the whole has been divided.

Maths Lab Activity

Aim: To understand the meaning of fractions by folding paper

Materials required:

(a) Paper cut-outs of shapes of a circle and a square (b) Colour pencils

Procedure:

1. Take a circle shape. Fold the circle into two equal parts. Fold the circle in such a way that the boundaries of the parts overlap with each other.

2. Unfold the paper and shade one part of the circle and write $\frac{1}{2}$ to represent one-half.

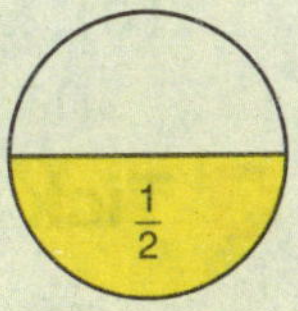

3. Take another circle shape (circle or square). Fold the shape into four equal parts.
4. Unfold the paper and shade two parts of the shape. Write $\frac{2}{4}$ to represent two-fourths.
5. Similarly, continue the process to show different fractions like $\frac{1}{4}$, $\frac{3}{4}$, etc.

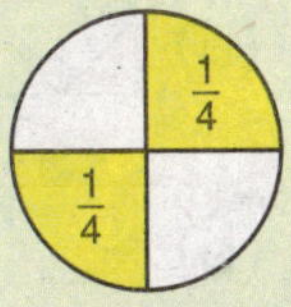

Conclusion: A fraction is a part of a whole.

Revision Exercise

1 **Write the fraction for the coloured parts. The first one has been done for you.**

Figure	Fraction	Figure	Fraction
(a) 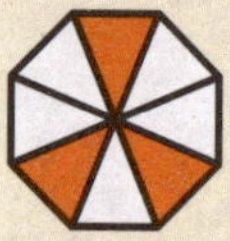	$\frac{3}{8}$	(e) 	—
(b) 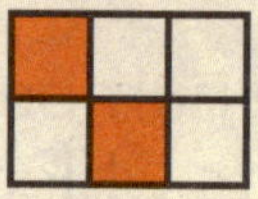	—	(f) 	—
(c) 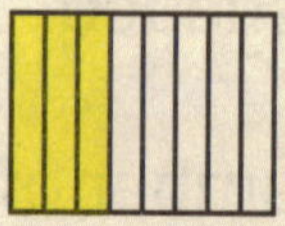	—	(g) 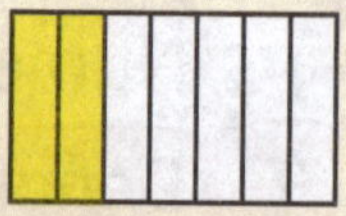	—
(d) 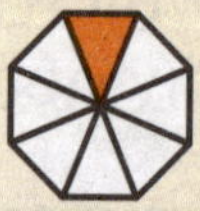	—	(h) 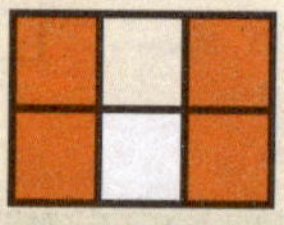	—

2 **Tick (✓) the shapes which represents $\frac{1}{2}$.**

(a)  ☐ (b)  ☐ (c) 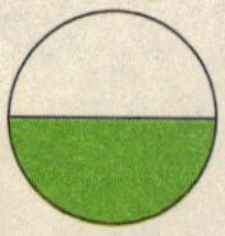 ☐ (d) 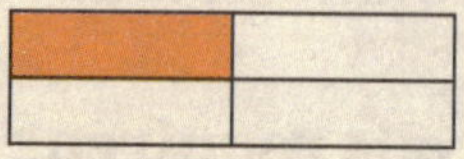 ☐

3 **Tick (✓) the shapes which represents $\frac{1}{3}$.**

(a)  ☐ (b)  ☐ (c) 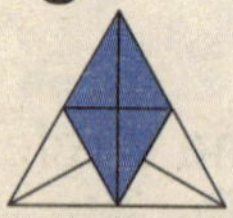 ☐ (d) 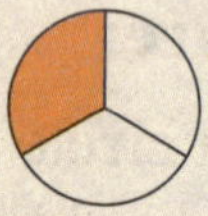 ☐

4 **Shade $\frac{1}{2}$ in red and $\frac{1}{3}$ in green in the following figures.**

(a) 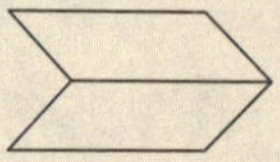 (b) 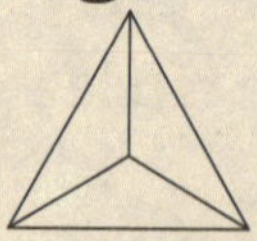 (c) 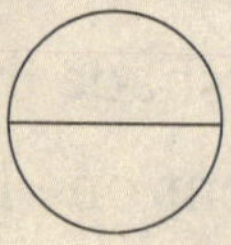 (d) 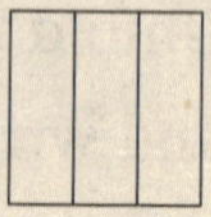

5 **Tick (✓) the shapes which show the representation of $\frac{1}{4}$.**

(a) 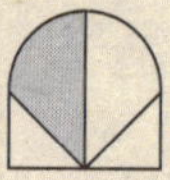 ☐ (c) 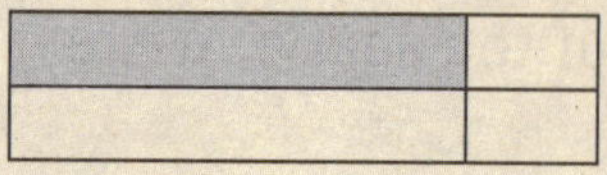 ☐ (e) 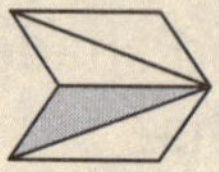 ☐ (g) 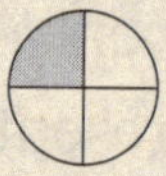 ☐

(b) 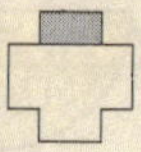 ☐ (d) 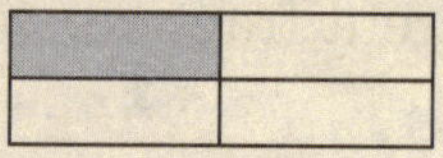 ☐ (f) 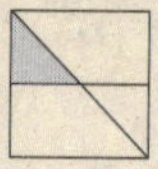 ☐ (h) 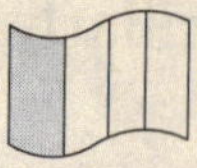 ☐

ASSESSMENT 2

Chapters 4-7

A Choose the correct option for each of the following.

1. Which of the following combination makes ₹10?

(a) 

(b) 

(c) 

(d) 

2. Jiya bought a chocolate for ₹20 and an ice cream for ₹15. If she had ₹50 with her, how much did she pay and how much is left with her?

(a) ₹35 and ₹25 (b) ₹35 and ₹15 (c) ₹15 and ₹35 (d) ₹25 and ₹15

3. Guddi has three notes of ₹50, two notes of ₹20, five notes of ₹10, nine coins of ₹5, four coins of ₹2 and six coins of ₹1 in her piggy bank. How much money does she have?

(a) ₹279 (b) ₹289 (c) ₹295 (d) ₹299

4. Which of the following clocks shows 7:30?

(a)  (b)  (c)  (d) 

5. The hour hand is missing from the clocks shown below. Choose the option that shows the correct position of the hour hand to show 11:30.

 : (a)  (b)  (c)  (d) 

6. Choose the correct order of the first four days of the week.
   (a) Monday, Tuesday, Thursday, Wednesday
   (b) Sunday, Monday, Tuesday, Wednesday
   (c) Sunday, Monday, Tuesday, Thursday
   (d) Monday, Tuesday, Wednesday, Thursday

7. Nayana and her friends are playing with the skipping rope. Read the table below and answer the questions.

Name	Number of Times
Nayana	24
Hari	9
Rita	15
Deepti	13

   i. Who skipped the most number of times?
      (a) Nayana (b) Hari (c) Rita (d) Deepti
   ii. If counted together, who skipped the same number of times as Nayana?
      (a) Hari and Rita (b) Hari and Deepti
      (c) Rita and Deepti (d) None of them

8. Raghav had ice creams and apples for five days as shown. Answer the questions that follow.

Monday	
Tuesday	
Wednesday	
Thursday	
Friday	

Raghav had only apples on ________ and only ice creams on ________ .
(a) Tuesday, Wednesday (b) Wednesday, Thursday
(c) Tuesday, Thursday (d) Thursday, Friday
Raghav had 5 ice creams on
(a) Monday and Tuesday (b) Tuesday and Friday
(c) Wednesday and Thursday (d) None of these

B Fill in the blanks.

1. You need ₹________ more to make ₹57 to ₹100.
2. A ball costs ₹15 and a bat costs ₹105. Srini has to pay ₹________ to buy both the items.
3. When it is 5:30, the hour hand is between ______ and ______ .
4. Look at the shapes drawn in the box and fill in the blanks.

   i. The number of ovals is ________ more than the number of circles.
   ii. There are ________ squares in the box.

C State whether the following statements are true (T) or false (F).

1. A dress costs ₹125. Pooja has two notes of ₹50 and four coins of ₹5. This amount is enough for Pooja to buy the dress. [ ]
2. Saturday is the last day of the week. [ ]
3. The following table shows the number of students in different classes. Study the table and state whether the statements that follow are true (T) or false (F).

Class	Number of Students
1	30
2	28
3	25
4	29
5	20

Class 1 has 5 students more than Class 3. [ ]
Class 4 has the least number of students. [ ]
Class 2 has 8 students less than Class 5. [ ]

4. Fraction is a part of a whole. [ ]

D Match the following.

Column A	Column B

This month has 31 days	
This month falls between May and July	February
This month comes just after January	April
	December
	June

COMPREHENSIVE ASSESSMENT

Chapters 1–7

A Choose the correct option for each of the following.

1. 9 × ____ = 72
   (a) 4 (b) 7 (c) 8 (d) 9
2. If divisor = 4, dividend = 32 and quotient = 8, the multiplication fact corresponding to the given information is
   (a) 32 ÷ 4 = 8 (b) 4 ÷ 32 = 8 (c) 4 × 8 = 30 (d) 4 × 8 = 32
3. The height of your classroom wall is about
   (a) 1 metre (b) 1 centimetre (c) 5 metres (d) 5 centimetres
4. In which of the following figures, the mugs have been arranged in the decreasing order of their capacities?
   (a)  (b) 
   (c)  (d) 
5. Which of the following objects has 4 corners?
   (a)  (b)  (c)  (d) 
6. Identify the missing shapes in the pattern shown below.
    ____ ____
   (a)  (b)  (c)  (d) 
7. What amount will Rohan need to buy these items?

   ₹125

   ₹35
   (a) 
   (b) 
   (c)  (d) 
8. Which of the following is written in the correct order?
   (a) January, February, April, March, June
   (b) October, November, December, February, January
   (c) August, September, October, November, December

(d) July, June, August, September, October

9. The table below shows the list of different books that Bittu has.

Type of Books	Number of Books
Comics	19
Storybooks	11
Activity books	5

Study the table and identify which of the following statements is true?

(a) The number of comics and activity books is the same as the number of storybooks. ☐

(b) The number of activity books and storybooks is the same as the number of comics. ☐

(c) The number of activity books and storybooks is more than the number of comics. ☐

(d) The number of activity books and storybooks is less than the number of comics. ☐

10. Given below is the list of items that Dina needs for the Maths project.

Item	Number of Items
Chart	2
Sketch pens	5 of different colours
Colour pencils	12 of different colours
Colour papers	3 of different colours

How many more colour pencils than sketch pens does Dina need for her project work?

(a) 12 (b) 7 (c) 17 (d) 5

B Fill in the blanks.

1. 100 ÷ 10 = ______

2. The division fact corresponding to the given number line representation is ____÷_____=_____.

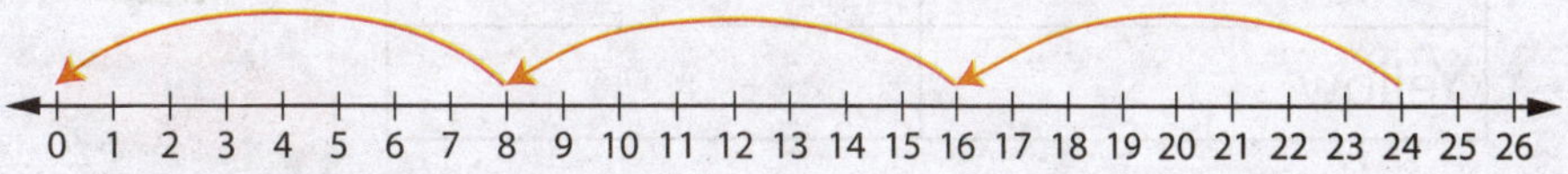

3. 1000 mℓ = ______ litre

4. In fraction $\frac{6}{7}$ the denominator is ______.

5. Look at the table below showing pastries of different type in a bakery shop and fill in the blank.

Pastry	Number of Pastries
Pineapple pastry	50
Chocolate pastry	70
Orange pastry	45
Strawberry pastry	48

The different types of pastries in the bakery are ______ .

C Answer the following questions briefly.

1. Write the multiplication facts corresponding to the division fact 35 ÷ 7 = 5.
2. Choose the correct unit and write it in the box given below the pictures.

   cm   m

Length of Vani's hair

Distance to Vani's school

3. Write the number of circles in each box. Identify the pattern and fill the empty box given below.

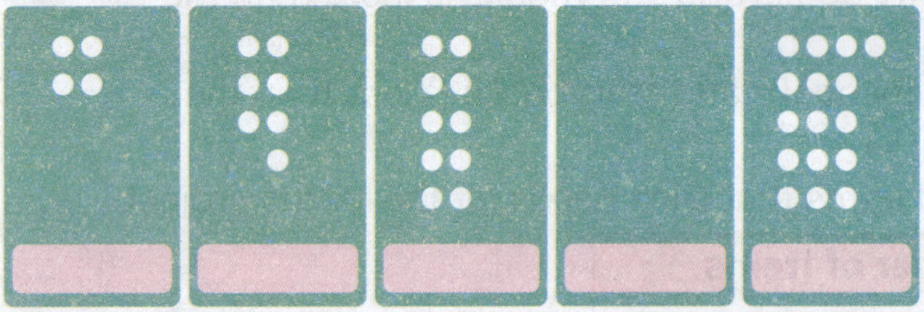

4. Rashi wants to buy a pen costing ₹35. She has a note of ₹20 and one note of ₹10. Will this amount be enough for her to pay for the pen? If not, then how much more money does she need?
5. Complete the table by counting the number of cars shown in the box below.

Colour of the Cars	Number of Cars
Red	
Pink	
Blue	
Yellow	

D Answer the following questions.

1. Solve the division problem 21 ÷ 7 using repeated subtraction and number line methods.
2. Write R if the right pan goes down, B if the pans are balanced and L if the left pan goes down.

3. Extend the following number patterns and write the rule for each pattern.

(a) 15, 20, 25, 30, ___, ___, ___

Rule: ______________________________

(b) 700, 650, 600, 550, ___, ___, ___

Rule: ______________________________

4. Draw the hour hand and the minute hand to show 1:30 in the clock shown here.

5. Some children decided to play different games on Sunday. They brought their toys. Complete the list of toys with the help of the following sentences.
Laila brought 3 soft toys. Rini brought 4 racing cars. Leena brought 1 board game and 2 skipping ropes. Bablu brought 1 flying disc and Chinky brought 3 balls. Rohit brought 2 balls and 5 racing cars.

Type of Toys	Number of Toys
Soft toys	
Racing cars	
Flying disc	
Balls	
Board game	
Skipping ropes	

E Answer the following questions in detail.

1. Given below is Nidhi's timetable for Monday. Answer the questions that follow.

She wakes up | Leaves for school | Comes home | Goes to play | Goes to bed

(a) What does Nidhi do at 7:00?
(b) What time does Nidhi go to play?
(c) When does Nidhi come home from school?
(d) What does Nidhi do at 8:30?
(e) When does Nidhi go to bed?

2. The cost of a pair of sports shoes in different shops is given below.
Footsteps – ₹450 Walk On – ₹300
Sports Star – ₹750 Shoe Star – ₹575
(a) Which shop should Asha buy from if she has ₹510?
(b) If Shiv has ₹850 and wants to keep ₹100 for himself, which shop should he buy from?
(c) Romila wants to buy one pair from Walk On and another pair from Shoe Star. She has ₹800. How much more money does she need?

ANSWERS FOR SELECTED QUESTIONS

Chapter 1

Exercise 1.1

1. (a) 2 2 2 2 2 2 Division Fact 12 ÷ 6 = 2
   (b) 3 3 3 3 3 Division Fact 15 ÷ 5 = 3
   (c) 4 4 4 4 4 4 Division Fact 24 ÷ 6 = 4
   (d) 5 5 5 5 5 5 5 Division Fact 35 ÷ 7 = 5
   (e) 7 7 7 Division Fact 21 ÷ 3 = 7
   (f) 5 5 5 5 5 Division Fact 25 ÷ 5 = 5

Exercise 1.2

1. (a) Division Fact: 10 ÷ 5 = 2 Number of boxes needed 2
   (b) Division Fact: 8 ÷ 2 = 4 Number of boxes needed 4
   (c) Division Fact: 15 ÷ 3 = 5 Number of boxes needed 5
   (d) Division Fact: 24 ÷ 3 = 8 Number of boxes needed 8
   (e) Division Fact: 40 ÷ 10 = 4 Number of boxes needed 4
   (f) Division Fact: 36 ÷ 9 = 4 Number of boxes needed 4
   (g) Division Fact: 16 ÷ 8 = 2 Number of boxes needed 2

Exercise 1.3

1. (a) 5 (b) 7
2. (a) 3 (b) 2
3. (a) 24 ÷ 8 = 3 (b) 21 ÷ 3 = 7

Exercise 1.4

1. (b) 9 × 2 = 18 and 2 × 9 = 18 (c) 6 × 6 = 36 and 6 × 6 = 36
   (d) 8 × 6 = 48 and 6 × 8 = 48 (e) 5 × 4 = 20 and 4 × 5 = 20
2. (a) 3 (b) 8 (c) 2 (d) 7 (e) 5
   (f) 3 (g) 3 (h) 7 (i) 9 (j) 8
   (k) 7 (l) 5 (m) 9 (n) 6 (o) 10

Exercise 1.5

1. (a) 27 ÷ 9 = 3 Dividend = 27 Divisor = 9 Quotient = 3
   (b) 24 ÷ 4 = 6 Dividend = 24 Divisor = 4 Quotient = 6
   (c) 30 ÷ 3 = 10 Dividend = 30 Divisor = 3 Quotient = 10
2. (a) 16 ÷ 8 = 2 (b) 30 ÷ 5 = 6 (c) Quotient = 9, 81 ÷ 9 = 9

Exercise 1.6

1. (a) 1 (b) 12 (c) 0 (d) 1 (e) 0 (f) 25

Exercise 1.7

1. Cost of one chocolate is ₹5
2. Cost of each ticket is ₹4
3. 16 spoons in each packet
4. 9 bulbs in each box

Revision Exercise

1. (a) 36 ÷ 6 = 6 (b) 40 ÷ 5 = 8
2. (a) 3 (b) 5 (c) 5
   (d) 4 (e) 7 (f) 10
3. (a) 3 (b) 3 (c) 6 (d) 2 (e) 4 (f) 9
4. (b) 9 ; 9 x 7 = 63 ; 7 x 9 = 63 (c) 4 ; 2 x 4 = 8 ; 4 x 2 = 8
5. 6 plants
6. 9 notebooks

Chapter 2

Exercise 2.1

The length of a butterfly — cm

The height of a ladder — m

The length of a door curtain — m

The length of your nose — cm

2. (a) m (b) cm (c) cm (d) m

Exercise 2.2

 g
 kg
 kg

Fruit Basket — kg

Marble — g

Football — g

Exercise 2.3

1. 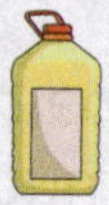 ℓ  ℓ  mℓ  mℓ

Revision Exercise

1. (a) 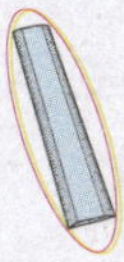 (b)  (c)  (d) 

2. (a) 

(b) 

(c) 

3.

Less	More	Less
More	More	Less

Chapter 3

Exercise 3.1

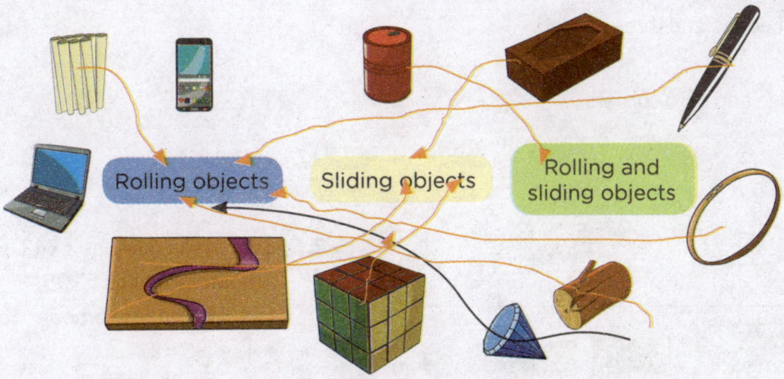

Exercise 3.2

Match the objects given below to the similar shape given in the box in the centre.

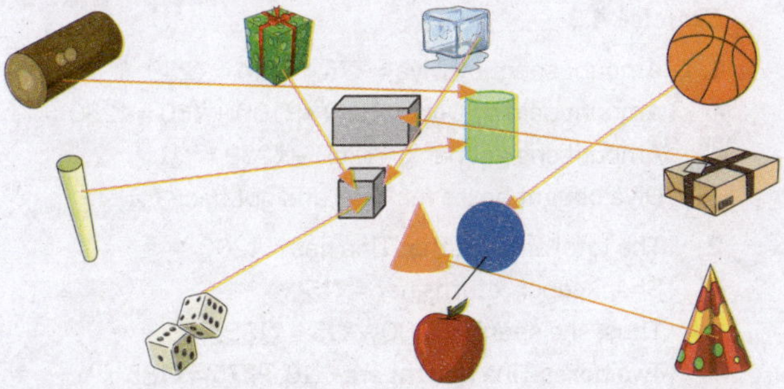

Exercise 3.3

Cone	Sphere	Cuboid	Cuboid

Cone	Cube	Sphere	Cylinder

Exercise 3.4

Object	Shape	Figure	Number of Edges	Number of Corners
	Square		4	4
	Triangle		3	3
	Oval		1	0

Object	Shape	Figure	Number of Edges	Number of Corners
	Rectangle		4	4
	Circle		1	0

Exercise 3.5

1. Follow instruction provided in the question

2. (a)  

(b)  

3. Follow instruction provided in the question

Exercise 3.6

(a) 10, 20, 30, 40, 50

(b) 14, 12, 10, 8, 6

Draw patterns by following the given patterns

Revision Exercise

1. **(a)** R and S **(b)** S **(c)** R

2.
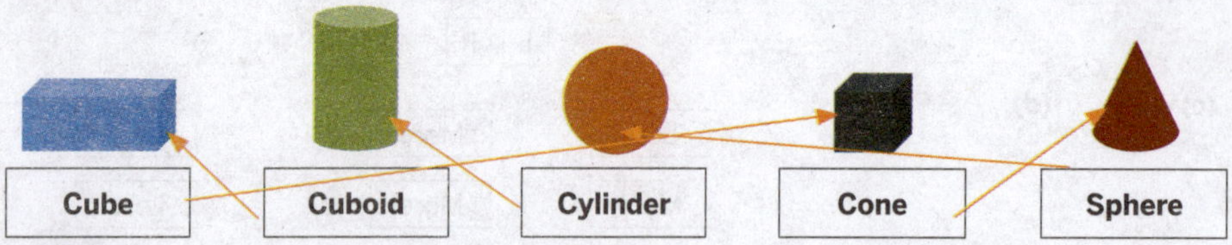

3.  One curved edge and zero corners

 Four straight edges and four corners

 Three straight edges and three corners

 One curved edge and zero corners

Chapter 4

Exercise 4.1

1.

2. Sum of the items she bought = 5 + 28 + 60 + 55 = 148
3. Vivek can buy Sketch Pen Set and Gel Pen for ₹50
   Cost of item1 = ₹35
   Cost of item 2 = ₹15
   Total Cost = ₹50

Exercise 4.2

1.

Item bought and amount paid	Amount returned
	₹2
	₹3
	₹15

2. Cost of the marbles = ₹42
   Amount Amit has = ₹35
   The difference in amount needed to buy the marbles
   = 42 – 35 = ₹7
3. Amount Latheef has = ₹77
   Amount he wants to make = ₹100
   Amount required = ₹100 – ₹77 = ₹23

Exercise 4.3

1. Amount spent by Diya = ₹75 + ₹164 = ₹239
   Amount paid by Diya = ₹100 + ₹100 + ₹50 = ₹250
   Amount she got back = ₹250 – ₹239 = ₹11
   Diya bought boxes for ₹239 and got back ₹11.
2. The total amount that Tina has = ₹200
   Shopkeeper returns her = ₹15
   Thus, she spent = ₹200 – ₹15 = ₹185
   Two boxes Tina bought are ₹110 + ₹75 = ₹185

Revision Exercise

1. **(a)** True **(b)** False
   (c) False
2. ₹35 
3. d **4.** ₹15

Chapter 5

Exercise 5.1

1. (a) 8:30 (b) 3:30
   (c) 10:30 (d) 1:30
2. (a) 1:30 (b) 9:30 (c) 11:30 (d) 4:30

3. (a) 7:00 (b) 7:30
   (c) 9:00 (d) 9:30
   (e) 11:30 (f) 12:00

Exercise 5.2

1. (a) Saturday (b) Wednesday
   (c) Sunday (d) Friday
3. (a) November (b) February
   (c) 5 (d) Saturday

Revision Exercise

1. (a) 10:30 (b) 4:30
   (c) 8:30 (d) 12:30
3. (a) ✗ (b) ✓ (c) ✗
   (d) ✓ (e) ✗
4. (a) March (b) February
   (c) October

HOTS

The number of weeks in a year 52
The number of days in a year 365
The number of weeks in a leap year 52
The number of days in leap year 366

Chapter 6

Revision Exercise

1. 

   (a) 5 (b) 1 (c) *Samosa*
2. (a) *Gulab Jamun* (b) *Rasgulla* (c) False
3. (a) Toys, Storybooks, Dresses, Shoes, Board games
   (b) 3 (c) 41

ENVIRONMENTAL STUDIES

1 Housing and Clothing

Learning Checklist

- Building materials and types of houses
- Types of roofs
- Good and clean house
- Clothes we wear

Let's Get Started

Let us take a look at Deepa's home. Fill in the missing letters in the boxes.

All of us need a house to live in. It protects us from heat, cold, wind and rain. We feel safe in our house.

Let us learn more about houses.

BUILDING MATERIALS AND TYPES OF HOUSES

Have you seen people building a house? Many people work together to build a house. They use different materials to build a house.

People building a house

A hut

Some houses are made from materials like grass, mud, bamboo, straw, ropes and sand. These houses are called ***kutcha* houses**. The most common *kutcha* house is a hut. *Kutcha* houses are commonly found in villages.

Some houses are made from materials like bricks, cement and steel. These houses are called ***pucca* houses**, for example, a bungalow. Nowadays, most of the houses in cities are *pucca* houses.

A bungalow

An igloo

Some houses are made from blocks of ice. Such houses are called **igloos**. They are found in very cold places.

TEMPORARY AND PERMANENT HOUSES

Some people keep moving from one place to another. So, they build houses that can be moved from place to place. These houses are called **temporary houses**. Following are the different types of temporary houses.

A tent

A yurt

Word Web

[1]**Canvas**: a strong, thick cloth
[2]**Gypsies**: people who travel from place to place

Tents and **yurts** are built with canvas[1] and bamboo. Tents are used as temporary shelter by armies and police. Yurt is a type of traditional tent used in some regions.

A caravan

A houseboat

A **caravan** is a house on wheels. It can be taken anywhere easily. It is used by gypsies[2].

A **houseboat** is a floating house which is made up of wood. We can find these types of houses in Kashmir and Kerala.

Know the Fact!

The houseboats found in Kashmir are usually fixed to the river bank.

People who stay at one place for a long time live in houses that are called **permanent houses**. These houses are very strong and cannot be moved from one place to another.

Following are the different types of permanent houses.

A cottage

A **cottage** is a small house made up of bricks and cement.

A bungalow

A **bungalow** is a large house with spacious rooms and lawns.

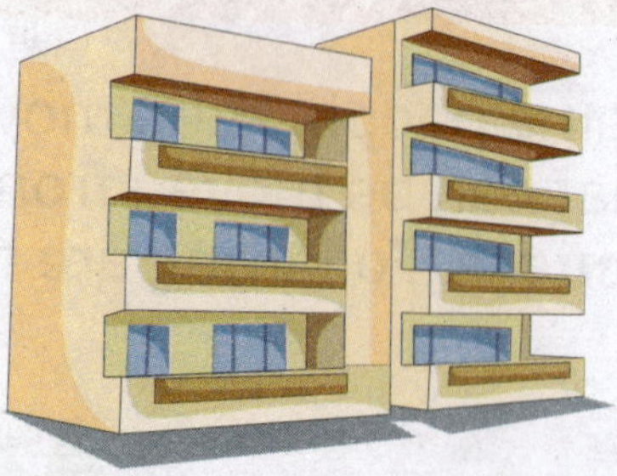

An apartment

An **apartment** is a multistoried building with many flats.

TYPES OF ROOFS

Different houses have different types of roofs. The roofs can be flat or sloping.

Houses in the hills have **sloping roofs**, while houses in the plains have **flat roofs**. People build houses on **stilts**[1] with sloping roof in the areas where it rains heavily so that the rainwater can easily fall from the roofs.

Word Web

[1]**Stilts**: strong wooden pillars that raise the level of the house above the ground or water

A sloping roof

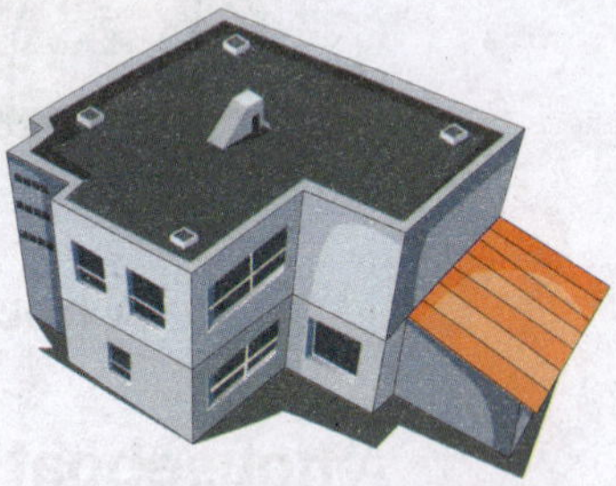

A flat roof

Sloping roof and stilts

GOOD AND CLEAN HOUSE

(a) A good house should be airy and get plenty of sunshine.

(b) We should keep our house neat and clean.

(c) The place around our house should also be kept clean.

(d) There should be trees and plants around our house.

Revise and recall

Fill in the blanks using correct words.

1. A hut is a __________ house. (*kutcha/pucca*)
2. Houses made up of materials like bricks, cement and steel are called __________ houses. (*kutcha/pucca*)
3. Igloos are made up of __________ . (bricks/blocks of ice)
4. Houses in the plains have __________ roofs. (flat/sloping)

CLOTHES WE WEAR

Clothes protect our body from heat, rain, wind and cold. They cover our body and make us look smart. We should always wear clean clothes.

We wear different clothes in different seasons.

We wear light cotton clothes on hot days as they keep our body cool.

When it rains, we wear a raincoat and gumboots, and carry an umbrella as they keep our body dry.

We wear woollen clothes in winter as they protect us from cold and keep us warm.

Let's Say Together

Kutcha houses

Pucca houses

Temporary houses

Permanent houses

Cotton clothes

Woollen clothes

Sing Along!

Clothing

Dresses are lovely and pretty,
We always like to wear,
We never wear if they are dirty,
Or if they have a tear.
Woollens for winter,
Cottons for summer,
Raincoats and umbrella for rainy days,
Protect us in all seasons.

Keywords

Temporary house: A house that can be moved from one place to another

Permanent house: A house that cannot be moved from one place to another

Igloo: A house made up of blocks of ice

Caravan: A house on wheels

Tent: A house made up of canvas and bamboo

Bungalow: A large house with spacious rooms

Apartment: A multistoried building with many flats

Summary

1. Different types of materials are used to build different types of houses.
2. People use materials like mud, bamboo, steel, cement, bricks, wood, grass and straw to build a house.
3. Temporary houses can be moved from one place to another.
4. Permanent houses are very strong and cannot be moved from one place to another.
5. Some houses have flat roofs, while some have sloping roofs.
6. Clothes protect us from the heat, cold, wind and rain.

EXERCISE

A Choose the correct answer for each of the following.

1. Which of the following materials is not used to build a *kutcha* house?
   (a) Cement (b) Bamboo (c) Straw (d) Grass
2. Which of the following is not a *pucca* house?
   (a) Yurt (b) Bungalow (c) Apartment (d) Cottage
3. Which of the following is a temporary house?
   (a) Bungalow (b) Caravan (c) Cottage (d) Apartment
4. In which of the following places do we find houseboats?
   (a) Chennai (b) Kashmir (c) Mumbai (d) Delhi
5. Which of the following do we wear during winter?
   (a) Cotton shirt (b) Raincoat (c) Sweater (d) Gumboots

B State whether the following statements are true (T) or false (F).

1. *Kutcha* houses are strong. ☐
2. A hut is made up of blocks of ice. ☐
3. A tent is a large building with spacious rooms and lawns. ☐
4. People build stilts with sloping roof in areas where it rains heavily. ☐
5. We wear woollen clothes in winter. ☐

C Match the following.

Column A	Column B
(a) A house on wheels	(1) Kashmir
(b) A traditional tent	(2) Hut
(c) A house made up of ice	(3) Caravan
(d) Houseboat	(4) Yurt
(e) A *kutcha* house	(5) Igloo

D **Give two examples for each of the following.**

1. Materials used to build a *kutcha* house ____________ ____________
2. Materials used to build a *pucca* house ____________ ____________
3. Permanent houses ____________ ____________
4. Types of roofs ____________ ____________

E **Replace the underlined word with the correct word from the box given below.**

Bungalow	Temporary	Kutcha	Igloo

1. Houses made from grass, mud and bamboo are called <u>pucca</u> houses. ____________
2. A house made from blocks of ice is called a <u>hut</u>. ____________
3. Tents and yurts are <u>permanent</u> houses. ____________
4. A <u>cottage</u> is a large house with spacious rooms and lawns. ____________

F **Answer the following questions briefly.**

1. Why do we need a house?

____

2. What is a houseboat?

____

3. What types of roofs do the houses in the following places have?

(a) Hills ____________

(b) Plains ____________

4. What do clothes protect us from?

____

G HOTS (Higher Order Thinking Skills)

Neha lives in Chennai. She is going to visit her friend in Kashmir during the month of December. Suggest the types of clothes that she should take with her to Kashmir.

(Hint: It is very cold in Kashmir during the month of December.)

H Fill in the missing letters to write the names of the objects shown.

___ R ___ ___ K S

T ___ ___ T

S ___ I ___ T S

C ___ R A V ___ N

I Project

What kind of a house would you like to live in—a caravan, a houseboat, a cottage or an igloo? Draw your house on a chart paper, colour it and display it in your class.

Identify and write 'P' for permanent house and 'T' for temporary house in the circles given below.

A cottage ◯

A caravan ◯

A tent ◯

A bungalow ◯

An apartment ◯

A yurt ◯

2 Air Around Us

Learning Checklist

- Wind
- What does air contain?
- Properties of air
- Keeping the air clean

Let's Get Started

Look at the pictures given below and answer the questions that follow.

What is filled in the balloons?

____

Why is the girl finding it difficult to walk?

____

Air is all around us. We cannot see or touch air, but we can feel it. All living things need air to breathe.

WIND

Moving air is called **wind**. Wind can help us in many ways.

(a) Wind moves a sailboat.

(b) Wind turns the blades of a windmill.

(c) Wind dries our wet clothes.

(d) Wind helps hot-air balloons to fly.

A gentle wind is called **breeze**. Leaves of a tree rustle[1] when a breeze blows.

A strong wind is called **gale**. Gales can blow off branches of trees.

A very strong and noisy wind is called **storm**. A storm can uproot trees and damage houses.

Word Web

[1]**Rustle**: to move with a soft sound

Gale

Storm

WHAT DOES AIR CONTAIN?

Have you seen water droplets on a bottle of cold water which is kept out of a refrigerator? Where do these water droplets come from?

This is because air contains water in the form of **water vapour**.

Air also contains small particles of dust and smoke. Smoke comes from vehicles, factories and burning things. This smoke mixes with the air.

Water droplets on a cold water bottle

Dust and smoke

Air also contains germs[1]. Germs get mixed with the air when a sick person coughs or sneezes.
Dust, smoke and germs make the air impure[2].

Revise and recall

Circle the correct option.

1. A very strong and noisy wind is called
   (a) breeze (b) gale (c) storm
2. Air contains water in the form of
   (a) solid (b) vapour (c) liquid

Word Web

[1]**Germs**: very small living things which can cause diseases

[2]**Impure**: dirty; not clean

PROPERTIES OF AIR

Air takes up space. When we blow air into a balloon, it fills the space inside the balloon.

Air filled in a tyre and football take up the space inside them and give them their shape.

Word Web

[1]**Inflate**: to fill something with air

[2]**Deflate**: to take the air out of an object filled with air

Air filled in a balloon

Air filled in a tyre

Air filled in a football

Air also has weight. Let us do an activity to see that air has weight.

Activity

Aim: To show that air has weight

Procedure:

(a) Blow two balloons so that they are about the same size.

(b) Tie the balloons using a thread.

(c) Tie each balloon on the ends of the ruler as shown in the figure.

(d) Tie a piece of thread at the centre of the ruler so that the ruler can be held parallel to the ground.

(e) Prick one balloon with a pin.

Observation: The ruler tilts in the direction of the inflated[1] balloon.

Conclusion: The balloon filled with air is heavier than the deflated[2] balloon. This shows that air has weight.

KEEPING THE AIR CLEAN

Dust, smoke and germs make the air dirty. Breathing dirty air can make us fall sick. We should breathe fresh and clean air to stay healthy.

We can keep the air fresh and clean by

(a) planting trees.
(b) walking or using a bicycle instead of other vehicles that produce smoke.

Children growing a plant

Children riding bicycles

Let's Say Together

Wind Breeze Gale Storm
Dust Smoke Germs

Keywords

Breeze: A gentle wind
Gale: A strong wind
Storm: A very strong and noisy wind

Summary

1. Moving air is called wind.
2. Wind helps us in many ways.
3. Depending on its speed, wind can be called a breeze, gale or storm.
4. Air contains water vapour, smoke, dust and germs.
5. Air takes up space and has weight.
6. We should breathe fresh and clean air for good health.

EXERCISE

A Fill in the blanks using correct words.

1. Branches rustle during a __________ . (storm/breeze)
2. Gale is a ____________ wind. (strong/gentle)
3. Your clothes will dry soon during ____________ weather. (windy/cold)
4. Air containing smoke is __________ . (clean/dirty)
5. Air takes up space and has __________ . (height/weight)

B Match the following.

Column A	Column B
(a) Breeze	(1) Smoke
(b) Water vapour	(2) Healthy
(c) Clean air	(3) Gentle wind
(d) Air fills	(4) Present in air
(e) Factories	(5) Space

C State whether the following sentences are true (T) or false (F).

1. Only human beings need air to breathe. ☐
2. Moving air is called wind. ☐
3. Air contains dust and smoke only. ☐
4. Air has weight. ☐
5. Plants and trees help to keep the air clean. ☐

D Name the following.

1. A gentle wind ______________
2. A strong wind ______________
3. Very strong and noisy wind ______________
4. Water is present in air in this form ______________

E Choose the odd one out.

1. Vehicles, Factories, Burning, Breathing
2. Breeze, Dust, Gale, Storm
3. Sail boat, Car, Hot air balloon, Windmill
4. Balloon, Tyre, Bat, Football

F Answer the following questions briefly.

1. What is wind?

   ____

2. Name two things which move with the help of wind.

   ____

3. Name two things filled with air.

   ____

4. Name three things that make air impure.

   ____

5. Write one thing we should do to keep air clean.

   ____

G HOTS (Higher Order Thinking Skills)

Why should we always cover our mouth while coughing or sneezing?
(Hint: Recall what does air contain.)

H Circle the things that use wind for moving.

I Project

Make a paper fan.

Take a square paper. Fold it back and forth as shown. Press and hold one end of the folded paper and spread the other. Your paper fan is ready!

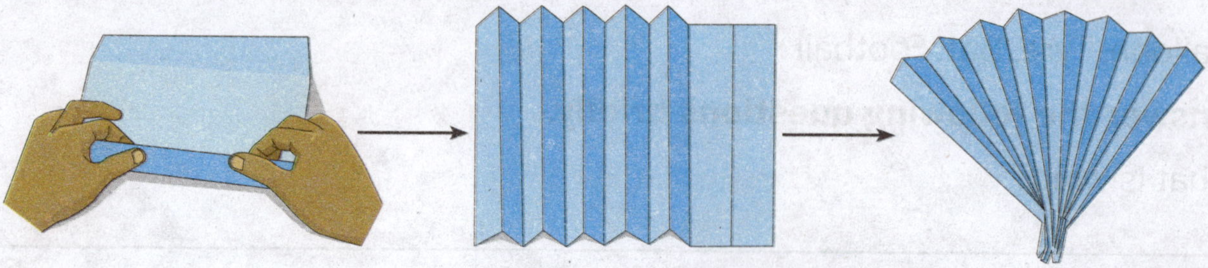

J Life Skills

We should breathe in clean air to stay healthy. Some things you can do to keep the air clean are given below:

(a) Plant a tree.
(b) Walk or use a bicycle instead of other vehicles.
(c) Do not burn things.

Pledge Card

I ______________, of Class ______________, pledge to ______________
(name)

______________________ to keep the air clean.
(activity)

WORKSHEET

A **Find the following words related to air in the box below. The first one has been done for you.**

VAPOUR	SMOKE	WINDMILL	BALLOON	CLEAN
STORM	DUST	KITE	BREEZE	HEALTH

Q	P	B	Q	G	D	V	V	J	G
D	A	R	S	H	U	K	A	C	Z
G	B	E	M	R	S	Y	P	L	W
P	A	E	O	R	T	K	O	E	I
G	L	Z	K	C	Z	Y	U	A	N
A	L	E	E	X	Z	F	R	N	D
H	O	S	T	O	R	M	R	W	M
F	O	K	I	T	E	N	O	W	I
A	N	H	E	A	L	T	H	U	L
K	W	C	N	E	I	M	G	Y	L

B **Fun Activity (Cross-curricular)**

Fill in the blanks using correct numbers.

(a) Wind can be of ______________ types—breeze, gale and storm.

(b) Water vapour, smoke, dust and germs are the ______________ things that air contains.

(c) Air has ______________ properties. It takes up space and has weight.

3 Water

Learning Checklist

- Where does water come from?
- How does water get dirty?
- Clean water for drinking
- Save water

Let's Get Started

Do you know who I am?

I fall from clouds as rain.

I flow from mountains as river.

I am dug out of the earth using a well.

I get collected in seas and oceans.

I am W ___ T ___ R!

Human beings, plants and animals—all need water to live. We need water for drinking, cooking, bathing, washing clothes, etc. Let us learn about water.

WHERE DOES WATER COME FROM?

Water comes down from clouds as rain. Rain is the main source of water. Rainwater fills up the rivers, lakes, ponds and seas. These are the other sources of water.

The water in the rivers, lakes, ponds and seas is called **surface water**. Canals and dams are built to make use of surface water.

Some amount of rainwater seeps[1] into the ground and gets collected as **groundwater**. We get groundwater from wells and hand pumps. Groundwater is mostly used for drinking purposes. In our homes, we get water from taps.

Canal

Tap

Hand pump

Word Web

[1]**Seep**: to flow slowly into something

STORAGE OF WATER

Storage of water means collecting water for future use. Water can be stored in tanks, tubs and buckets.

Wonder!

Only a very small amount of water on the Earth can be used for drinking.

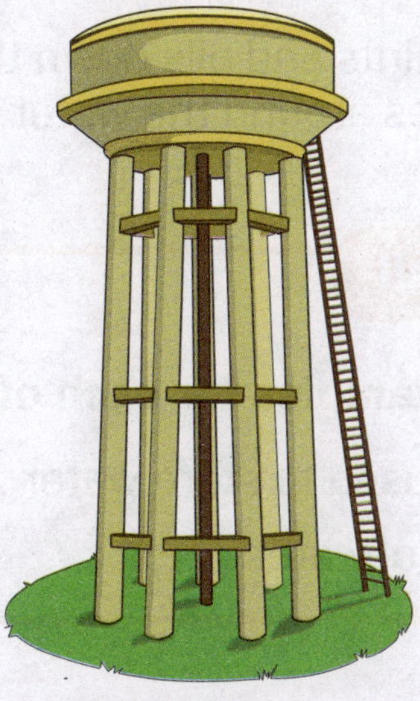

Water tank

Bucket

HOW DOES WATER GET DIRTY?

Water in ponds, lakes and rivers may not be clean. The following picture shows how river water gets dirty.

River water getting dirty

Using dirty water is not good for health. You can help to keep the water clean in the following ways.

(a) Never throw waste into ponds, rivers, lakes and seas.
(b) Do not throw paints and oils down the sink.
(c) Plant lots of trees around the water bodies.

Revise and recall

Give two examples for each of the following.

1. Vessels used to store water __________ __________
2. Sources of water __________ __________

CLEAN WATER FOR DRINKING

Groundwater is not safe for drinking. This water contains germs which can make us fall sick.

To kill the germs, we should always boil water before drinking.

We should always drink clean water. The container in which water is stored should always be covered.

Drinking water

SAVE WATER

Did you know that only a very small amount of water on the Earth can be used by people? Rest of the water is either salty or in the form of ice. So, it is important not to waste water and save as much as possible. Following are the simple things that you can do to save water.

(a) Do not leave the water tap open while brushing your teeth.

(b) Tell an adult when you see a leak in a water pipe.

(c) Collect and use rainwater for gardening.

Science in Context
The method of collecting and storing rainwater is called rainwater harvesting.

Let's Say Together

Rainwater Surface water Groundwater Drinking water

Keywords

Surface water: The water in the rivers, lakes, ponds and seas

Groundwater: The rainwater that seeps into the ground

Summary

1. The water in the rivers, lakes, ponds and seas is called surface water.
2. The rainwater that seeps into the ground is called groundwater.
3. Water can be stored in tanks, tubs and buckets.
4. We should always boil water before drinking.
5. It is important not to waste water and save it for future use.

EXERCISE

A Fill in the blanks using correct words.

1. Water comes down from clouds as ________________. (snow/rain)
2. Water in ________________ is an example of surface water. (wells/rivers)
3. ________________ are built to use surface water. (Canals/Tanks)
4. Dirty water is ________________ for drinking. (safe/not safe)
5. We should not ________________ water. (waste/collect)

B State whether the following statements are true (T) or false (F).

1. We get groundwater from rivers. ☐
2. Ponds are one of the sources for groundwater. ☐
3. Groundwater can be stored by building dams. ☐
4. Dirty water contains germs. ☐
5. We should not throw waste into the water bodies. ☐

C Write one word for each of the following.

1. It fills up ponds, lakes, rivers and seas ____________
2. We get water from this in our homes ____________
3. We get groundwater from this ____________
4. We do this to kill germs in water ____________

D Give two examples of the following.

1. Ways to keep water clean

   (a) ____

   (b) ____

2. Ways to save water

   (a) ____

   (b) ____

E Answer the following questions briefly.

1. What is surface water?

   ____

2. How is groundwater formed?

   ____

3. Why should we boil water before drinking?

   ____

4. Where do we store water?

   ____

5. Why should we not waste water?

   ____

F HOTS (Higher Order Thinking Skills)

Explain why we should not drink water directly from a river.
(Hint: Think about how river water gets dirty.)

G **We need to save water by making sure that the taps are closed properly when not in use. Help Raj turn off the leaky tap.**

H **Life Skills**

(a) Drinking water should be stored in clean vessels.

(b) Containers with drinking water should be covered.

(c) It is our duty to save every drop of water.

Tick (✓) the dos and cross out (✗) the don'ts.

Rakesh always drinks water from the container that is covered.

☐

Amit does not care whether the water container is covered or open.

☐

I **Fun Activity (Cross-curricular)**

Nancy uses 3 mugs of water for brushing, 7 mugs for watering her plants, 11 mugs for washing her bicycle and 2 mugs for washing her hands. How many mugs of water does she use in total?

WORKSHEET

Unscramble the following words related to water. Use the pictures given below for clues. One has been done for you.

1. verir ___river___
2. could __________
3. ianr __________
4. analc __________
5. kindrgni __________
6. lewl __________
7. lboingi __________

1 

2 

3 

4 

5 

6 

7 

4 Forms of Water

Learning Checklist

- Water exists in different forms
- Water cycle

Let's Get Started

Look at the following pictures and complete the sentences given below using the correct words.

(1) The girl is adding ____________ to the glass of juice. (water/ice)

(2) In earlier days, trains used to run on ______________ . (ice/steam)

(3) Rivers and ponds are filled with ________________ . (water/steam)

Water is present on the Earth in different forms. Steam and ice are also forms of water.

Let us learn how water changes into steam or ice.

WATER EXISTS IN DIFFERENT FORMS

What happens when water is heated?

When we heat water in a vessel, it starts boiling and we see bubbles forming in the water. These bubbles then rise and come out as **steam** or **water vapour**. When this steam comes in contact with a cold plate, it cools down and turns back into drops of water.

When boiled, water changes into steam

When cooled, steam changes into water

What happens when you put water in the freezer?

The water will slowly get colder. Finally, the water will change into **ice**. When you take this ice out of the freezer, the ice will change into water. This is because it is hotter outside than in the freezer.

So, water changes from one form to another when it is heated or cooled. Ice, water and water vapour or steam are the three different forms of water.

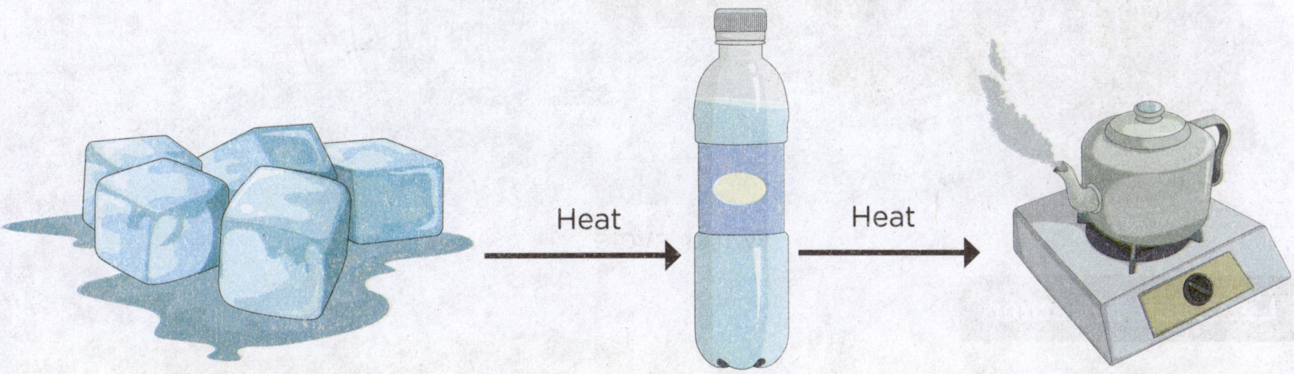

WATER CYCLE

Have you ever wondered where water comes from and where it goes?

The sun heats up the water in seas, rivers, lakes and ponds which changes into **water vapour**. This water vapour rises up into the air where it cools and changes into tiny droplets of water. These water droplets join together to form **clouds**.

When these clouds become heavy with water drops, they fall on the Earth as **rain**. Rainwater fills up ponds, lakes, rivers and seas again and the cycle continues.

This cycle in which water rises up from the water bodies as water vapour, forms clouds and then falls as rain is known as **water cycle**.

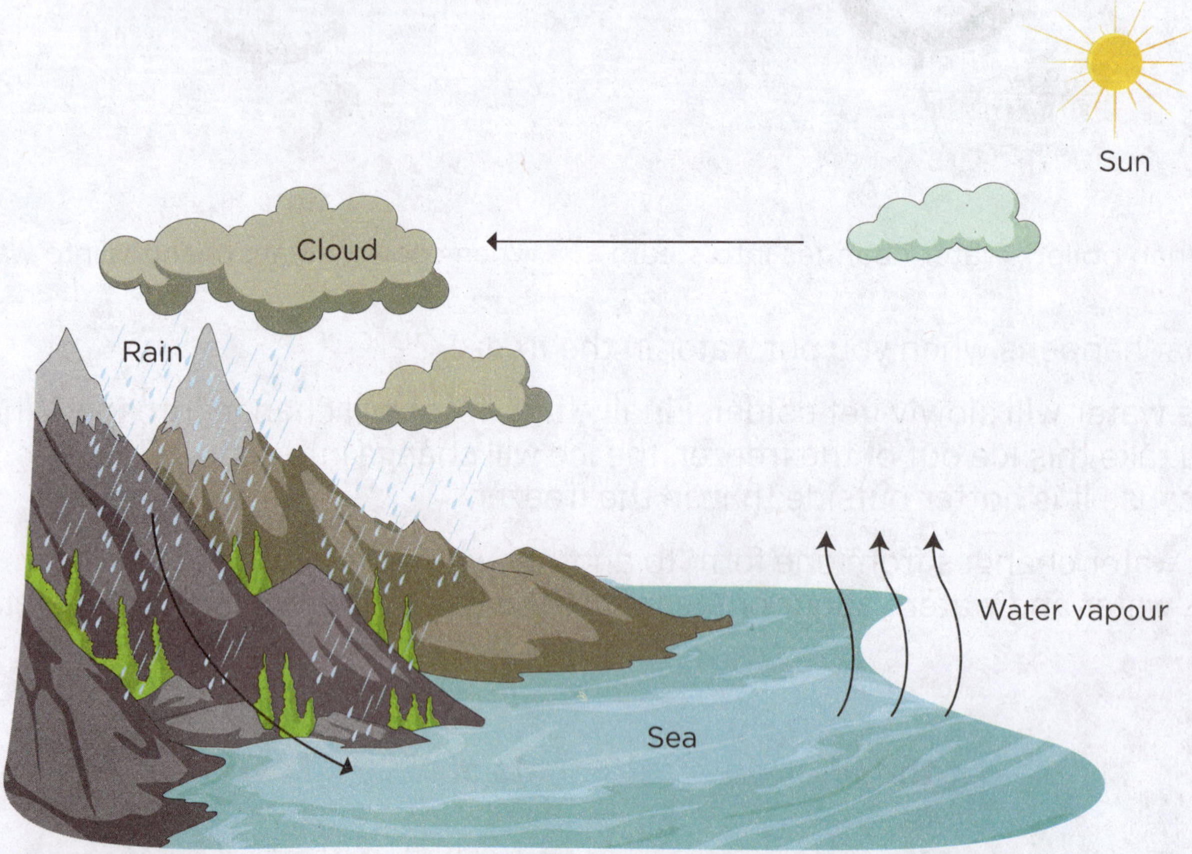

Water cycle

Let's Say Together

Water Water vapour Ice Cloud Rain Water cycle

Keywords

Water cycle: The cycle in which water rises up from the water bodies as water vapour, forms clouds and then falls as rain

Cloud: Tiny drops of water formed in the air when water vapour is cooled

Summary

1. Water changes from one form to another when it is heated or cooled.
2. Water exists in three different forms: ice, water vapour and water.
3. When water is heated, it rises up into the air as water vapour. When this water vapour is cooled, it forms tiny drops of water which join together to form clouds.
4. When the clouds become heavy, they fall on the Earth as rain.
5. The cycle in which water rises up from the water bodies as water vapour, forms clouds and then falls as rain is called water cycle.

EXERCISE

A Fill in the blanks using correct words.

1. Water rises as steam when it is ____________ . (heated/cooled)
2. Steam turns into drops of water when it comes in contact with ____________ surface. (hot/cold)
3. Water, steam and ____________ are the three different forms of water. (water vapour/ice)
4. Clouds are made up of ____________ . (ice/water drops)

B State whether the following statements are true (T) or false (F).

1. We cannot see water drops in the air. ☐
2. Water changes into ice when it is heated. ☐
3. Water exists in two different forms. ☐
4. The cycle in which water rises up from the water bodies as water vapour, forms clouds and then falls as rain is called water cycle. ☐

C Match the following.

Column A	Column B
(a) Boiling	(1) Heats the water in seas
(b) Clouds	(2) Water changes into steam
(c) Freezing	(3) Water changes into ice
(d) Sun	(4) Tiny water drops joined together in air

D Who am I?

1. I am formed by boiling water. ____________
2. I am formed by putting water in a freezer. ____________
3. I heat the water in the oceans into water vapour. ____________
4. I am formed when water drops join together in the sky. ____________
5. I fall from clouds and fill rivers, ponds and lakes. ____________

E Replace the underlined word with the correct word from the box given below.

Ice	Water vapour	Drops

1. Sun heats the water in the water bodies to form <u>clouds</u>. ____________
2. When clouds become heavy with water <u>vapour</u>, they fall on earth as rain. ____________
3. Water forms <u>bubbles</u> on freezing. ____________

F Answer the following questions briefly.

1. When does water change from one form to another?

____

2. Name the three forms of water.

____

3. What happens when we boil water?

____

4. How are clouds formed?

____

5. What happens when clouds become heavy with water drops?

____

G HOTS (Higher Order Thinking Skills)

1. Can you think of things other than water that change their form on heating or cooling?
   (Hint: Oils and milk products)
2. On which days will the most amount of water turn into water vapour—sunny days, cold days or rainy days?
   (Hint: The sun heats up water to form water vapour.)

H Identify and write the form of water.

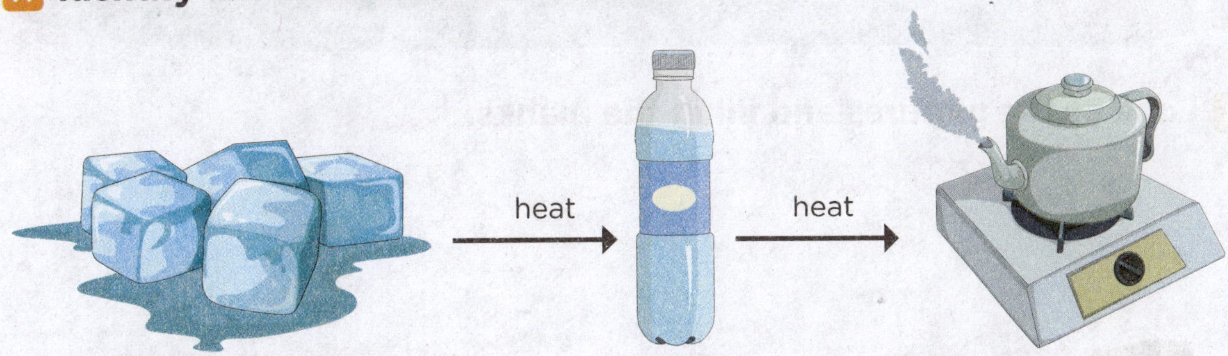

_______________ _______________ _______________

I Project

Make your own cloud. (Note: Do this only with the help of an adult.)

1. Fill a clear 1-litre plastic bottle one-third with warm water.
2. Ask an adult to light a matchstick and drop it in the bottle.
3. Close the bottle with the cap tightly.
4. Squeeze the bottle and then release it.
5. A cloud will appear on releasing and dissappear on squeezing.

WORKSHEET

A **Draw arrows to complete the water cycle and label the diagram.**

B **Look at the pictures and fill in the blanks.**

When boiled, water changes into ________________.

When cooled, steam changes into ________________.

5

Rocks and Minerals

Learning Checklist

- Types and uses of rocks
- Minerals

Let's Get Started

Given below are two famous buildings in India made of different types of stones. Can you write the name of the buildings and the colour of the rocks used to make them?

Name ______________________ ______________________

Colour ______________________ ______________________

TYPES AND USES OF ROCKS

Our Earth is mostly made up of hard solid material called **rocks**. Rocks form the outer surface of the Earth. They are very huge stones. There are different types of rocks found on hills, mountains and valleys. Rocks are also found at the bottom of rivers and seas.

Rocks can be of different colours, shapes and sizes. Some rocks are rough to touch while some are smooth.

Rough rock

Smooth rock

Hard Rocks

Some rocks are very hard to break. They are called **hard rocks**. Granite, marble and sandstone are some examples of hard rocks.

Granite

Marble

Sandstone

Granite is a very hard rock. It is found in white, pink or light grey colour.

It can be polished smooth and is mainly used for making floor tiles, kitchen slabs and walls of buildings.

Marble is also a hard rock which can be cut into small pieces. It is found in several colours and patterns.

It is used for making buildings, floors of houses, decorative items, etc.

The Taj Mahal in Agra is built using white marble. The Jaipur City Palace in Rajasthan is built using pink-coloured marble.

Sandstone is not as hard as granite and marble. It is used for making buildings and statues. The Red Fort and Jama Masjid in New Delhi are built using sandstone.

Know the Fact!

The Taj Mahal is one of the seven wonders of the world.

Jama Masjid

Soft Rocks

Some rocks are soft and break easily. They are called **soft rocks**. Coal, slate and chalk are examples of soft rocks.

Coal is found deep below the surface of the Earth. It is black in colour. Coal is used to produce electricity, for cooking and as a fuel to run steam engines.

Slate tiles are used as roofs for buildings. They are also used to make writing slates and blackboards for children.

Chalk is used to write on blackboards. It is also used to make beautiful carvings[1].

Coal

Slate

Chalk

Word Web

[1]**Carving:** a design made by cutting rocks

Science in Context

The natural process that breaks rocks into smaller pieces is called **weathering**.

Revise and recall

Match the following.

(a) Taj Mahal	(1) Slate
(b) Red Fort	(2) Blackboard
(c) Coal	(3) Sandstone
(d) Chalk	(4) White marble
(e) Soft rock	(5) Used for cooking

MINERALS

All rocks are made up of minerals. Minerals are of different colours and sizes. Some are hard, some are soft and some are shiny. We use things made of minerals every day.

> **Wonder!**
>
> There are about 2000 different kinds of minerals.

(a) The **salt** that we use in our food is a mineral.

(b) **Quartz** is the most commonly used mineral. It is used in watches.

(c) **Diamond** used in jewellery is a mineral. It is also used for cutting glasses. It is the hardest known mineral.

(d) **Talc** is used for making talcum powder. It is the softest mineral.

(e) **Graphite** is used in pencil leads.

(f) **Mercury** is used in thermometers.

Gemstones

Gemstones are hard and colourful minerals. They are cut into different shapes and polished to make them shine. They are used to make jewellery. Emerald, ruby and corals are some examples of gemstones.

Emerald

Ruby

Let's Say Together

Rocks	Granite	Marble	Sandstone	Coal	Slate
Chalk	Minerals	Diamond	Quartz	Graphite	Talc
Salt	Mercury	Gemstone	Ruby	Emerald	Coral

Summary

1. The Earth is made up of different types of rocks.
2. Rocks differ in shape, size and colour.
3. Some rocks are hard and some are soft.
4. Marble, sandstone, coal and chalk are some of the types of rocks.
5. Rocks are made of minerals.
6. We use things made of minerals in our daily lives.
7. Gemstones are hard and colourful minerals.

Keywords

Rocks: The hard solid materials with which the Earth is made
Minerals: Substances with which all the rocks are made
Gemstones: Hard and colourful minerals

EXERCISE

A Fill in the blanks using correct words.

1. Slate is a type of ______________ rock. (hard/soft)
2. ______________ is used for cooking. (Marble/Coal)
3. ______________ is used to write on blackboards. (Slate/Chalk)
4. Diamond is the ______________ mineral. (hardest/softest)
5. Gemstones are ______________ minerals. (soft/hard)

B Match the following.

Column A	Column B
(a) Salt	(1) Gemstone
(b) Coal	(2) Mineral used in food
(c) Marble	(3) Produce electricity
(d) Ruby	(4) Talcum powder
(e) Talc	(5) Used as flooring

C State whether the following statements are true (T) or false (F).

1. Marble is used to make floorings. ☐
2. Jama Masjid is built using sandstone. ☐
3. All minerals are of the same colour and size. ☐
4. We use things made of minerals in our day-to-day life. ☐
5. Gemstones are used to make tiles. ☐

D Name the rock or mineral.

1. It is a mineral used in watches ____________
2. It is mostly used to make kitchen slabs ____________
3. It is used as a fuel to run steam engines ____________
4. It is used for cutting glasses ____________
5. It is used in pencils as lead ____________

E Give two examples of the following.

1. Gemstones

   ____________ ____________

2. Minerals

   ____________ ____________

3. Hard rocks

   ____________ ____________

4. Soft rocks

   ____________ ____________

F Answer the following questions briefly.

1. What are rocks?

   ____

2. Where can we find rocks on the Earth?

   ____

3. Give any two uses of coal.

____

4. Give any two uses of slate.

____

G HOTS (Higher Order Thinking Skills)

Why are gemstones used for making jewellery and not graphite or coal?
(Hint: Think about the property of gemstones that makes them suitable for making jewellery.)

H Identify and write the name of the rock/mineral from which these objects are made.

Blackboard

____

Ring

____

Pencil lead

____

I Project

Observe the picture given. The pebbles are arranged in shapes that resemble footprints. In the same way, collect different types of small pebbles or rocks and arrange them into any shape you like.

A **Find the following words in the word box. One has been done for you.**

GRANITE	CORAL	DIAMOND
GRAPHITE	GEMSTONE	TALC
QUARTZ	ROCKS	SLATE

G	E	M	S	T	O	N	E	B	J
A	F	N	T	A	L	C	F	O	H
K	Y	B	J	G	C	O	R	A	L
D	I	A	M	O	N	D	L	Z	Q
G	R	A	P	H	I	T	E	G	U
V	Q	A	D	D	E	H	K	O	A
G	R	A	N	I	T	E	K	M	R
S	L	A	T	E	H	A	S	F	T
M	T	C	X	C	E	D	S	I	Z
R	O	C	K	S	P	R	S	T	T

B **Fun Activity (Cross-curricular)**

Solve the puzzle with the help of the picture clues.
(Note: All the answers have the word 'ROCK' in it.)

1. One who performs in a show is called a ______________
2. Kids have fun in riding on this toy ______________
3. It is a kind of fire cracker ______________

1

2

3

6 Light and Shadow

Learning Checklist

- Sources of light
- Shadow

Let's Get Started

Look at the pictures given below. Put a tick mark (✓) against the objects which give out light and a cross mark (✗) against the objects that do not give out light.

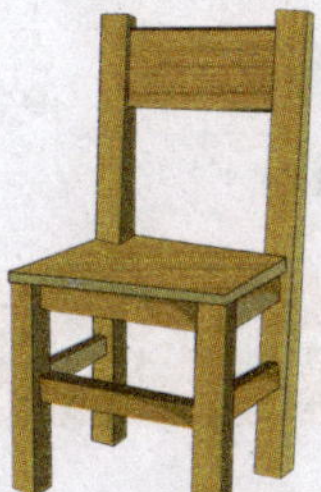

Light helps us to see things around us. We cannot see in the dark. We can see things only when there is light.

SOURCES OF LIGHT

Objects which give out light are called **light sources**.

Light sources are of two types: **natural** and **man-made** or **artificial**.

Natural light sources: Objects found in nature that give out light are called natural sources of light. Examples of natural source of light are sun and stars.

Sun

Star

Science in Context

A flying insect called firefly gives out light from its tail that shines in the dark.

Man-made (artificial) light sources: Man-made objects that give out light are called man-made or artificial sources of light. Examples of artificial source of light are candle, bulb and lantern.

Candle

Bulb

Lantern

Revise and recall

Fill in the blanks using correct words.

1. Light helps us to ____________ things. (see/move)
2. Objects that give out light are called ______ sources. (light/dark)
3. There are ____________ types of light sources. (four/two)
4. Objects found in nature that give out light are called __________ sources of light. (natural/artificial)
5. Man-made objects that give out light are called ______________ sources of light. (natural/artificial)

SHADOW

When light is not allowed to pass through an object, a **shadow** is formed. It always appears as a dark patch on the opposite side of the light source.

Shadow of a child

Shadow of a tree

Activity

Aim: To form a shadow

Materials required: A football, a torch and a screen

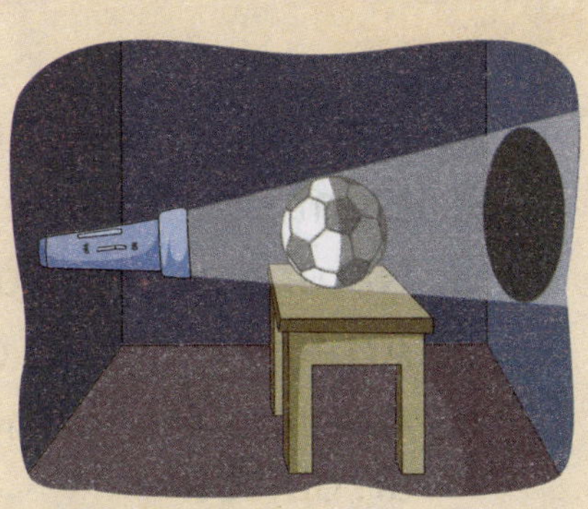

Procedure:

1. Take the football, the small torch and the screen to a dark room.
2. Hold the ball in one hand and the torch in the other hand such that the ball is in between the torch and the screen.
3. Switch on the torch such that the light falls on the ball.

Conclusion: You will see the shadow of the ball on the screen.

The length of a shadow is different at different times of a day. Shadows are long in the morning and evening, while short at noon.

Let's Say Together

Light   Light source   Natural source   Man-made source   Shadow

Keywords

Light source: Objects that give out light
Natural light source: Objects found in nature that give out light
Artificial light source: Man-made objects that give out light
Shadow: A dark patch formed when light is not allowed to pass through an object

Summary

1. Any object that gives out light is called a light source.
2. Light sources are of two types—natural and artificial.
3. Natural sources of light are found in nature.
4. Artificial sources of light are man-made objects that give out light.
5. A shadow is formed when the light is not allowed to pass through an object.
6. A shadow is always formed on the opposite side of the light source.
7. Shadows are long in the morning and evening and short at noon.

EXERCISE

A Choose the correct answer for each of the following.

1. Which of the following is a light source?
   (a) Candle   (b) Water   (c) Mirror   (d) Sky
2. Which of the following is a natural light source?
   (a) Bulb   (b) Candle   (c) Sun   (d) Lantern
3. Short shadows are formed during ____________ .
   (a) morning   (b) evening   (c) noon   d) night
4. Shadows are always __________ in colour.
   (a) bright   (b) white   (c) dark   (d) red

B **Fill in the blanks using correct words.**

1. Both candle and sun are the sources of . (light/sound)
2. Bulb is __________ source of light. (a natural/ an artificial)
3. When light falls on an object, its __________ is formed on the opposite side of the light source. (colour/shadow)
4. To form a shadow of an object, __________ is a must. (darkness/light)

C **State whether the following statements are true (T) or false (F).**

1. Light helps to see things around us. ☐
2. Natural light sources are made by humans. ☐
3. Shadow appears as a dark patch. ☐
4. Shadows are always of the same length. ☐

D **Write one word for each of the following.**

1. Objects that give out light __________
2. An artificial source of light __________
3. The part of the day when shadows are the shortest __________
4. The colour of a shadow __________

E **Choose the odd one out.**

1. Candle, Bulb, Star, Lantern
2. Book, Pencil, Chair, Torch
3. Buib, Sun, Star, Firefly

F **Answer the following questions briefly.**

1. Why do we need light?

____

2. What are the two types of light sources?

____

3. Name two man-made sources of light.

____

4. When is a shadow formed?

____

G HOTS (Higher Order Thinking Skills)

Can the shadow of an object be formed in a dark room? Why or why not?
(Hint: What is a must thing to form a shadow?)

H Tick (✓) the picture showing the correct way of shadow formation.

☐

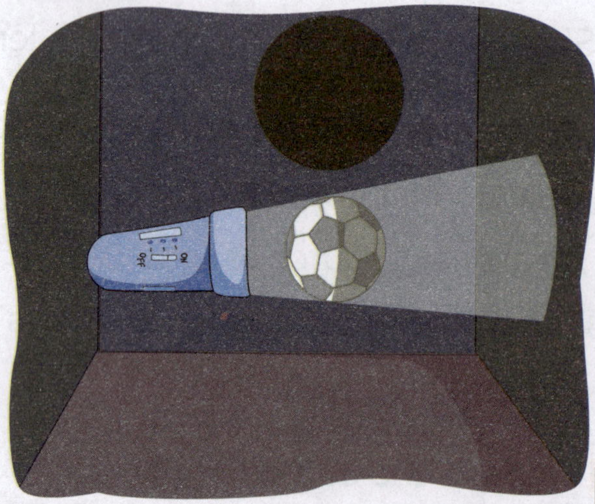

☐

I Project

Take any four different objects (a pen, a pencil, an eraser, a book, a stick) and a white paper. Make each object stand on the paper one by one and expose it to a light source. Trace the shadow of each object one by one.

WORKSHEET

A Match the objects in Column A with their shadows in Column B.

Column A	Column B
(a) 	(1) 
(b) 	(2) 
(c) 	(4) 
(d) 	(4) 

B Mention what source of light you would prefer to use in each of the following cases.

1. In the morning ____
2. At night ____

A **Fill in the blanks with the given words:**

warm   protect   cotton   raincoat   cool

1. Cotton clothes keep us __________.
2. Clothes __________ us from heat, cold and rain.
3. Woollen clothes keep us __________.
4. We use __________ when it rains.
5. We wear __________ clothes in summer.

B **Match the picture with the word.**

	Breeze
	Storm
	Gale

C **Pick out water-related actions. One has been done for you.**

(Washing)	Breathing	Swimming	Splashing	Drinking	Dancing
Boiling	Walking	Reading	Sleeping	Bathing	Pouring

D **Arrange the given words in the sequence of water cycle.**

Rain Water Clouds Water vapour

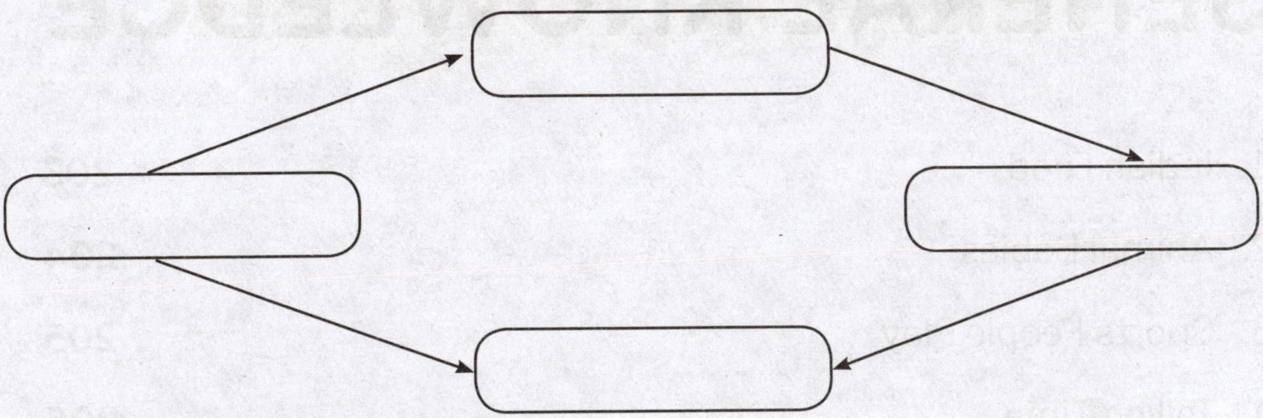

E **Write the names of these rocks:**

1. A red rock used for building ______
2. A black rock found under the Earth ______
3. A rock which is used in jewellery ______
4. A rock we can write on ______

F **Look at the light sources. Label it as 'N' if it is natural light source and label it as 'A' if it is artificial light source.**

 ☐	 ☐
 ☐	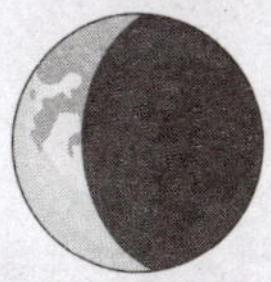 ☐
 ☐	 ☐

GENERAL KNOWLEDGE

1 Indian Food

Use numbers 1, 2, 3 ... for the letters of the alphabet to decode the names of these types of Indian food given below. One has been done for you.

A	B	C	D	E	F	G	H	I	J	K	L	M
1	2	3	4	5	6	7	8	9	10	11	12	13
N	O	P	Q	R	S	T	U	V	W	X	Y	Z
14	15	16	17	18	19	20	21	22	23	24	25	26

2	9	18	25	1	14	9
B	I	R	Y	A	N	I

4	8	15	11	12	1

16	1	18	1	20	8	1

4	15	19	1

2 Animal Babies

Look at the pictures. Complete the names of the animal babies.

1. 
sheep

L__ __ __

2. 
dog

P__ __

3. 
goat

K__ __

4. 
cow

C__ __ F

5. 
cat

K__ TT __ N

6. 
horse

F__ A __

Fact Zone

A baby kangaroo is called joey.

3 Sports People Play

Identify the sports people play. Choose the correct word from the box to name the sports.

1.

____

2.

____

3.

____

4.

____

5.

____

6.

____

Parachuting	Kayaking	Surfing
Handball	Snorkeling	Mountain Biking

Fact Zone

Adventure sports which can be dangerous are known as Extreme Sports.

4 Telling Time

Read the time shown in these clocks. Arrange the activities in the correct order, starting from morning to evening. Write 1,2,3... in the boxes next to them.

1\.

Time: 2:15 p.m.
Rohan eats lunch at home.

2\.

Time: 1:00 p.m.
He goes home from school.

3\.

Time: 5:10 p.m.
He goes to the park to play.

4\.

Time: 7:25 a.m.
He gets into the school bus.

5\.

Time: 10:10 a.m.
Rohan has a sandwich.

6\.

Time: 12:00 noon
He is in school.

7\.

Time: 9:00 p.m.
He goes to bed.

8\.

Time: 6:00 a.m.
Rohan wakes up.

9\.

Time: 3:45 p.m.
He does his homework.

5 Taking Care of My Body

Tick (✓) the actions that you should do and cross out (×) those that you should not do to take care of your body.

1\.

2\.

3\.

4\.

6 At School

Tick the correct habits and cross out the careless habits followed at school.

1.

Raise hand to answer question

2.

Feel sad for friend's win

3.

Keep school clean

4.

Keep sitting when teacher enters class

5.

Help friend in lessons he missed as he was ill

6.

Make noise when there is no teacher

7.

Sneak out of a school event

8.

Not help since you are not in the play

Fact Zone

A boarding school is a school where students study and live while studying.

7 Counting Shapes

Count the shapes in the ship and write their names.

Triangle Square Circle Star Rectangle

8 Things We Use

We use objects made from many things daily. Match these objects with their source.

1.

2.

3.

a. Wood

b. Hen

c. Jam

d. Wood Pulp

e. Honey

f. Butter

g. Tea

4.

5.

6.
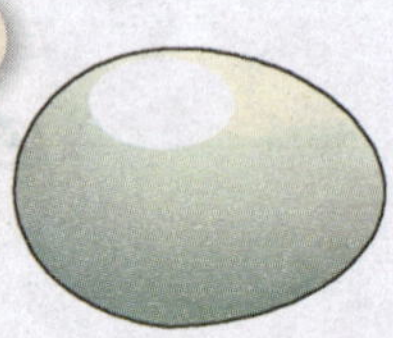

7.

Fact Zone

Glass is made from sand.

9 Sportspeople of India

Match these sportspeople of India with their names.

1. 

2. 

3. 

4. 

5. 

6. 

a. Vijender Singh

b. Suresh Raina

c. Abhinav Bindra

d. Mahendra Singh Dhoni

e. Saina Nehwal

f. Sushil Kumar

Fact Zone

Dhyan Chand, India first and finest Hockey player, helped to win the gold medal in the Olympics in 1928, 1932 and 1936.

•10 Directions

Look at the map of India and circle the correct answer.

1. Jammu and Kashmir is located in south/north India.
2. Gujarat is located in east/west India.
3. Assam lies in the north-west/north-east direction in India.
4. Kerala lies in the south/west of India.
5. Odisha is located in the west/east.

11 Uses of Computer

Computer is used in many places today. Look at the pictures and name the places where it is used.

1. 

____

2. 

____

3. 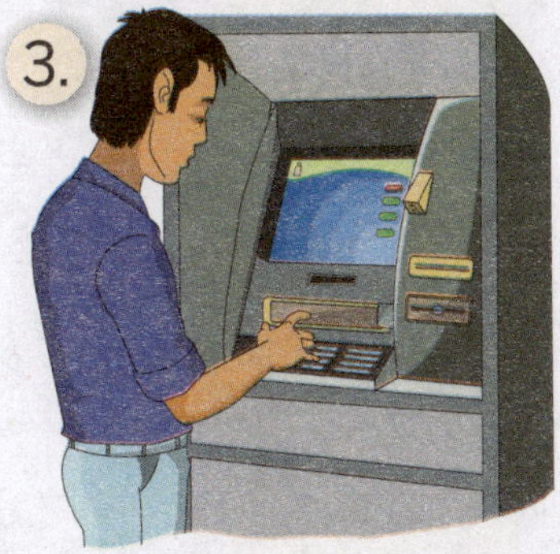

____

4. 

____

5. 

____

6. 

____

Fact Zone

Computer was invented by Charles Babbage.

12 Word Formation

Complete the word grid using the help box.

______	ROT	
RA	______	
CAB	______	E
ZUC	______	I
TO	______	O
S	______	ACH
O	______	
P	______	
MU	______	D
______	______	
PI	______	PLE

BAG

CAR

CHIN

EAR

DISH

MAT

KIN

PIN

PUMP

STAR

RANGE

13 Clean Environment

Tick the environment-friendly actions and cross out the careless actions.

Fact Zone

World Environment Day is celebrated on 5 June every year.

14 Sea Animals

Look at the pictures and complete the crossword with the names of some sea animals.

Fact Zone

Dolphins sleep at night with one eye open, just under the surface of water and come to the surface occasionally to breathe.

A **Match the following.**

1. 

2. 

3. 

4. 

5. 

6. 

a. Sushil Kumar

b. Careless action

c. In hospitals

d. Crab

e. Rafting

f. Wood

B **Tick the correct answer.**

1. A cow's baby is called a ________________ (Calf/Foal)
2. Rohan wakes up at ________________ (6:00 am/9:00 am)
3. Butter is made from ________________ (Egg/Milk)
4. Standing up when teacher enters the class is a ________________ habit (good/bad)
5. Assam is located in the ________________ direction in India. (north-east/north-west)
6. Complete the word: BAS _ _ _ (KET/KEP)

1 Paul and the Picnic

Discuss

Look at the pictures. Talk about them in class.

Read along

Paul woke up late every day. He took a lot of time to bathe and dress and was always late to the breakfast table. He would never reach school on time. His teacher scolded him for being late. But Paul did not care.

One day, Paul's teacher told the class that they were to go for a picnic from school the next day. Paul was very excited! He loved picnics. Paul's teacher told everyone to reach the school at 8:00 a.m. The bus would leave exactly at 8:15 a.m. Knowing that Paul was always late, his teacher told him, especially, to be punctual.

Paul asked his mother to wake him on time. Next morning, his mother woke him. As usual, he did not get up and was late. Even though his father dropped him to school, he reached only at 8:20 a.m. By then, the bus had left with all his classmates and there was nobody in his class.

Think and Say

Your alarm clock has stopped working. How can you still wake up on time?

Paul was very sad. He returned home crying. His mother made him sit on her lap. She wiped his tears and then spoke to him gently. 'Paul, this has happened because you have made it a habit to be late. What do you think you should do?' She asked.

'Mother, I know it is my fault. I promise you and myself that I will never be late again,' he said.

From that day onwards, Paul got up early every morning. He was never late for school again.

Figure out

Tick (✓) the correct options to complete the sentences.

1. When Paul woke up late
   a. he reached school late and was scolded by his teachers. ☐
   b. he could not attend lessons. ☐
2. Paul missed the picnic because
   a. he could not reach school on time. ☐
   b. he did not want to go for the picnic. ☐
3. Paul was sad because
   a. he did not do well in his subjects. ☐
   b. he missed the picnic. ☐

4. What did Paul realize?
   a. He realized that he should make it a habit to be on time. ☐
   b. He realized that missing lessons is a good habit. ☐
5. At the end, Paul changed his habit. List four good things that would have happened to Paul had he always been on time.
   a. ______________________________
   b. ______________________________
   c. ______________________________
   d. ______________________________

Relate

Choose the best answer. Draw a smiley against it.

1. Your friend and you are supposed to go for a birthday party. Your friend is late. What would you do?

a. Get angry and shout at him

b. Help him understand why it is important to be on time

2. Your friend misses classes because he is late and asks for your notebook to take down the notes. What would you do?

a. Do not give him the notebook

b. Give him the notebook and make him promise not to be late again

3. You are late for a movie with your friends. Because of this everybody misses the movie. Your friends get angry. What would you do?

a. Ignore my friends

b. Say sorry to my friends

Create

Following a timetable is very important. Make a clock with your daily routine and hang it in your room. Follow it strictly to ensure that you are never late for anything.

You need

- A sheet of coloured chart paper
- Scissors
- Coloured markers
- Ribbon
- Compass

Steps

1. Draw a big circle on the chart paper and cut it out.
2. Divide the circle into 24 equal parts.
3. Write the time and the activity that you do in that time slot in the different parts of the circle.
4. Decorate it as you like.
5. Fold the ribbon in a loop and paste it at the back of the circle.

Hang it in your room and follow it every day.

Remember

- Get up early.
- Plan a daily timetable and follow it.
- Pack your bag according to the class timetable before going to bed.
- Keep your school dress on a hanger with shoes and socks ready before going to bed.
- Set your clock ahead of time by 5–10 minutes. This will help you to be on time.

Enjoy

Read the story *Black and White* about being on time. You could look up the Internet to find the story.

Be smart

1. Arrange these ten words related to time in alphabetical order.

second	hour	calendar	clock	year
minute	day	month	week	time

1. ____________ 2. ____________

3. ____________ 4. ____________

5. ____________ 6. ____________

7. ____________ 8. ____________

9. ____________ 10. ____________

2. Here is a game that you and your friends can play with your teacher to practise completing work on time.

   Divide your class into teams of four children each. Your teacher will give you a number of cards with the letters of the alphabet on them. Your teacher will also give you a time limit. Make as many words as you can using all the letter cards.

   The team which makes the most number of correct words, in the time given, wins the game.

3. Observe people around you. Make a list of activities and people who follow a set time for work.

______________________	______________________
______________________	______________________
______________________	______________________
______________________	______________________
______________________	______________________

Teaching tips

- Tell students how being late affects the schedule of other people.
- Stress on how so many other people have to be on time so that students can attend classes.
- Talk about how students' parents have to leave for work or get up on time.
- Give examples of activities and people who follow a set timetable for work.

2 Rats! Rats! Rats!

Discuss

Look at the pictures. Talk about them in class.

Read along

Little Aimol loved playing pranks.

He would tease everyone and play pranks on them. He would also lie to his family. He would scare his sister by saying, 'Look at the rats under your bed! They will bite you at night.' His sister would get scared and cry.

One day, his grandmother was boiling soup. Aimol took a spoonful and said, 'Yuck! No salt.' His grandmother mixed some more salt into it though she had, in fact, put salt in it earlier. That evening, nobody could have the salty soup!

Another day, he told his father, 'Dad, your car has been stolen!' His dad ran out instantly. The car was found right in the middle of their driveway. Inside the house, Aimol was rolling on the carpet, laughing so hard that his stomach hurt.

One night, Grandfather decided to tell him the story of the shepherd boy who played a prank by shouting, 'Wolf! Wolf!'

'So, when the wolf really came, and the boy shouted "wolf", nobody believed him,' said Grandfather. But Aimol only laughed when Grandfather finished the story, and went off to sleep.

Think and Say

Your friend is asking you to play a prank on another friend. What would you do?

That night, something strange happened. Aimol heard some screeching noises and woke up with a startle. It was dark. The noises were coming from under his bed. He peeped and was horrified! There were rats and rats and rats under his bed. He shouted, 'Mum! Dad! Rats! Rats!' But, nobody came.

Aimol jumped from his bed and ran to the living room. Everyone sat there, chatting. He said, 'Come quickly! There are rats under my bed!' Nobody even looked at him. Aimol shouted again, 'I am not lying. Please believe me!' Nobody even bothered to get up.

'Aimol! Aimol!' called someone. Aimol opened his eyes. It was Grandfather.

Aimol sat up. 'The rats?' he said.

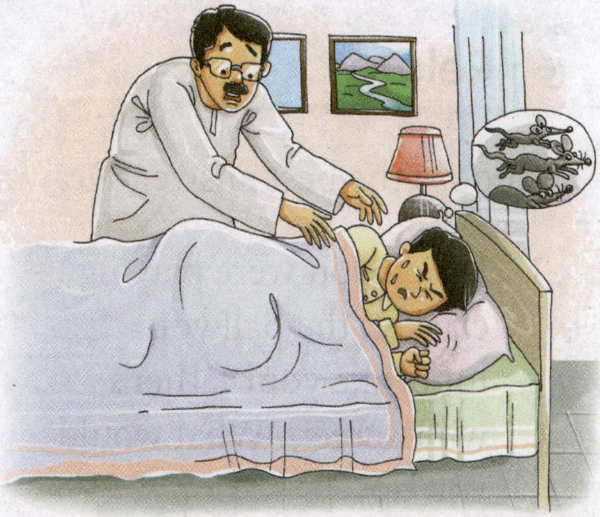

'What rats?' his grandfather asked, 'You were shouting in your sleep. Did you have a bad dream?'

'So all those rats were a dream!' Aimol sighed with relief. From that day, Aimol decided never to tell lies again. And, never did he play pranks on anyone to trouble them either.

Figure out

Tick (✓) the correct options to answer the questions.

1. Do you think scaring someone as a prank is fun?
   a. Yes. It is fun! ☐
   b. No. It is not fun. ☐
2. Do you think Aimol could have found a better way to spend his time?
   a. No. Playing pranks is a good hobby. ☐
   b. Yes. Aimol could have spent his time more wisely. He could have read books or painted pictures or even learnt to play an instrument. ☐
3. Do you think that Aimol's dream actually taught him a lesson?
   a. Yes. Aimol needed to realize that lying is bad. ☐
   b. No. Aimol continued to play pranks. ☐

4. Do you think Grandfather told the story of the boy who cried 'Wolf!' to Aimol on purpose?
    a. Yes. So that Aimol could learn from the story. ☐
    b. No. He just told him a story. ☐
5. Do you think Aimol will play more pranks in future?
    a. Yes. I think so. ☐
    b. No. I do not think so. ☐

Relate

Choose the best answer. Draw a smiley ☺ against it.

1. When you were playing cricket, the ball you hit broke your father's windscreen. What would you do?

a. Confess to Father about the windscreen

b. Hide and lie to him if he asks

2. Last night, you were sleepy and could not finish your homework. What would you tell your teacher?

a. Lie to your teacher and tell her that you were ill

b. Tell your teacher the truth

3. You have broken your brother's toy. What would you do?

a. Tell him that you broke his toy, and say sorry

b. Hide the broken toy

Create

Find a poem on being honest. Write it on a piece of chart paper. Hang it in your room. Read it every day and remind yourself to have a truthful day ahead.

Remember

- Lying is a bad habit.
- Lying can hurt people.
- If you always lie, no one will believe you when you speak the truth.
- Being truthful is a good quality. We must practise it.

Enjoy

Read the story *The Boy Who Cried Wolf!* Discuss the story in class.

Be smart

Write two words that mean the opposite of the words 'lie' and 'truth'.

Lie	Truth
______________	______________
______________	______________

Teaching tips

- Tell the students about the concepts of honesty and dishonesty, and include examples such as cheating and bribing.
- Stress on ways to make better use of time, such as working on a hobby.
- Tell the students about the rewards and consequences of being honest and dishonest. Tell them that we are responsible for the results of our actions.

Project I: The Mystery Box

Six people can play this game at one go.

Make teams of three each. Name the teams A and B.

Take an old shoe box with a lid. This can be made into a mystery box.

Group A places some things in the box. Make sure Group B does not see them.

Groups A and B have to stand facing each other. Place the mystery box in the centre, between the two groups.

Let one person from Group A describe a thing that has been placed in the box by giving examples and talking about it. The person has to be careful not to say the name of the thing. The person from Group B, standing in the opposite direction, will have to guess the thing.

For example, if Marie of Group A has placed a toy plane inside the box, she may say:

It flies in the sky.

We can go from one place to another in it.

Continue playing the game till all the members of the groups have had a chance. Only three hints are allowed. If the child from Group B cannot guess the object in three hints, it means that the two students need to work on cooperating and try again at a later date.

At the end, judge how many pairs could cooperate well to complete the task.